THE MARK OF THE BEAST REVEALED

The real meaning of your credit score

Dr. Spart A. Cuss

iUniverse, Inc.
Bloomington

The Mark of the Beast Revealed
The real meaning of your credit score

iUniverse books may be ordered through booksellers or by contacting:

iUniverse
1663 Liberty Drive
Bloomington, IN 47403
www.iuniverse.com
1-800-Authors (1-800-288-4677)

ISBN: 978-1-4620-1524-5 (sc)
ISBN: 978-1-4620-1525-2 (ebook)

Printed in the United States of America

iUniverse rev. date: 06/14/2011

The Mark of the Beast Explored

What is the meaning of the mark of the beast mentioned in the prophetic book now known as Revelation? Was the mark a code for a Roman emperor from long ago who persecuted the early church? Or is it a code to identify some dictator who will rule the world one day? Advances in technology include tiny implantable transponders already used to identify livestock. Books and websites can be found which offer a grim picture of a near future where earth's people are marked with a technological device such as transponder or barcode. Perhaps the warning from Revelation means we ought to fear having our medical records encoded onto a chip we wear under our skin as a part of some future health care reform? Were any of these the concerns on John's mind when he penned the biblical book we call Revelation?

The number 666 lifted from a manuscript penned in the first century has been popularized in films and books until it has attained the status of an icon for American pop culture. There is even an internet web site devoted to films using the number 666. Because of its use in pop culture, people with no biblical literacy at all associate the number 666 with the Antichrist, the personification of evil. As with any other literary work, it is best to begin with the context itself to understand the author's intent. John writes in Revelation 13:16-18.

> *And he causes all, the small and the great, and the rich and the poor, and the freemen and the slaves, to be given a mark on their right hand or on their forehead, and he provides that no one will be able to buy or to sell, except the one who has the mark, either the name of the beast or the number of his name. Here is wisdom, let him who has understanding calculate the number of the beast, for the number is that of a man; and his number is six hundred and sixty-six.*

Incredible as it may seem the value of the number might not specifically be 666. Very ancient manuscripts give alternate renderings for the number, 616 or 656. Bits and pieces of an ancient copy of the text were found along with half a million other fragments of papyri in 1895 by two Oxford archaeologists in the ancient Egyptian city of Oxyrhynchus. The papyri fragments were packed up and shipped off to England where they sat in storage for a hundred years until advances in technology made it feasible for scholars to reconstruct the fragment of Revelation that includes the section from 8:3 to 15:7. Based on well accepted principles, experts in the science of analyzing writing styles dated the manuscript bits to the late third or early fourth century. This makes the passage even more ancient than the Codex Sinaiticus from which we get then value 666 for the mark. The Oxyrhynchus manuscript gives the value of number as 616.The variant reading came as no surprise to scholars as early church fathers such as Irenaeus had mentioned it.

The ancient Greeks were fascinated with numerology and assigned numbers to words and phrases by the process of adding up number values assigned to Greek letters. Since the original manuscripts of the New Testament were first written in Greek, this method of interpretation has a long history. Some numerologists concluded the number 666 was a code for Emperor Nero who ruled the Roman Empire from 54 to 68 AD. Using numerology a little differently, and beginning with the number 616, others have concluded it stood for Emperor Caligula who ruled from 37 to 41 AD. If the number is a code for the name of some long dead Roman despot, we moderns need not concern ourselves with John's meaning. Apart from historical interest, the number would be irrelevant for our time. Likely because of this, modern proponents of numerological interpretations use a variety of other methods of numerology to produce modern despots. This effort includes one web site that identifies the current prince of the United Kingdom as the designated ruler. If one wishes to sell books on the popular market, it makes at least financial sense to update the culprit identified in John's work.

Sir Isaac Newton offered very sage advice regarding efforts to interpret ancient historical books that we do well to heed. According to him, prophetic books such as Daniel and Revelation were written in order to provide assurance to those readers who would live through the events written about by the prophets. In other words, such books were not intended to allow people to foresee the future, but to let the readers understand that God foresaw the unfolding of His plan from ancient times. It was this truth that was to provide readers comfort.

If we strip away the layers of interpretation that have been added over the years, we gain perspective useful for our time. It would be odd indeed if the mark of the beast stood for the so-called Antichrist in this book as such a being is not mentioned in Revelation, a fact established by consulting any exhaustive concordance or online search engine. Elsewhere in the bible the same author wrote that many antichrists had already appeared in the world by the first century. It would be best to begin our quest for the meaning of the mark by giving up the notion it stands for the mythic figure of the Antichrist made famous by Hollywood. By getting rid of this presupposition, we might actually come to understand what John intended us to know.

Looking to the context of the passage, we learn the mark has a function. It facilitates commercial transactions. People are given a mark so they may engage in buying and selling. In this passage, people seem to have no choice about the mark, it is given to them by the beast who marks everyone, rich and poor, great and small, slave and free. Later in Revelation we read a proclamation that includes the conditional preposition, *if*, which implies choice in a matter related to the mark.

> *Then another angel, a third one, followed them, saying with a loud voice, "If anyone worships the beast and his image, and receives a mark on his forehead or on his hand, he also will drink of the wine of the wrath of God..."*

Worshipping the beast is a theme addressed in passages throughout John's prophecy, including: 14:11, 16:2, 19:20, and 20:4. Contrasted with worshipping the beast and his image is attaining victory over the beast as in Revelation 15:2.

> *And I saw something like a sea of glass mixed with fire, and those who had been victorious over the beast and his image and the number of his name, standing on the sea of glass, holding harps of God. And they sang the song of Moses, the bond-servant of God, and the song of the Lamb, saying, Great and marvelous are Your works,*
> > *O Lord God, the Almighty;*
> > *Righteous and true are Your ways,*
> > *King of the nations!*

> *Who will not fear, O Lord, and glorify*
> *Your name?*
> *For You alone are holy;*
> *For all the nations will come and worship*
> *before you,*
> *For Your righteous acts have been revealed.*

In one passage we read that the beast marks everyone, but later we learn that not everyone worships the beast who marked them. Some people are victorious over the beast because they will not worship the beast, instead they worship the Lord.

The concept of choice is so central to scripture that it runs from the very first chapters of Genesis where man is presented with a choice between two trees through the final prophetic book. It is a prominent theme in the history of the nation of Israel, a people confronted with a stark choice about worship (Deuteronomy 11:16-20.)

> *Beware that your hearts are not deceived and*
> *that you do not turn away and serve other gods*
> *and worship them. Or the anger of the LORD*
> *will be kindled against you, and He will shut*
> *up the heavens so that there will be no rain*
> *and the ground will not yield its fruit; and you*
> *will perish quickly from the good land which*
> *the LORD is giving you. You shall therefore*
> *impress these words of mine on your heart and*
> *on your soul; and you shall bind them as a sign*
> *on your hand, and they shall be as frontals on*
> *your forehead.*

Economic prosperity for agrarian people like the ancient Israelites depends on the weather. God here warns His nation they would face severe economic repercussions if they choose to worship or serve other gods. Note that the passage warns them not to allow themselves to be deceived and led astray. The local deities worshipped by the people and nations surrounding the Israelites were often fertility gods and goddesses. These deities were worshipped because they offered material prosperity to their devotees. The pages of the Old Testament are an extended lesson on the Israelites attempting to worship these deities along with the LORD, which made God Almighty quite angry at His people. He instructed his people to impress His words of warning about worship on their heart and soul, binding them as a sign on their hands and forehead. This passage gives us a clue; because this is where the beast places his mark on people. Notice the passage from Deuteronomy quoted above says these words will serve as a sign. A sign is used to convey information about facts, conditions or qualities. God wanted His people to carry an outward sign of the condition of their hearts and souls. God is offended when people worship the works of their own hands. See for example Jeremiah 1:16, "*I will pronounce My judgments on them concerning all their wickedness, whereby they have forsaken Me and have offered sacrifices to other gods, and worshiped the works of their own hands.*"

Worshiping Idols

Worship is a theme central to both the New and Old Testaments. Literally, worship is bowing down in homage, adoration or fear before the object which is worshipped. Jesus offered this wisdom to his followers on the subject (Matthew 6:23-25):

> *No one can serve two masters; for either he will hate the one and love the other, or he will be devoted to one and despise the other. You cannot serve God and Mammon. For this reason I say to you, do not be worried about your life, as to what you will eat or what you will drink; nor for your body, as to what you will put on. Is not life more than food and the body more than clothing?*

Notice the contrast here, Jesus does not say it will be difficult to serve God and Mammon, he says it is impossible. Mammon in this passage is personified as an object of worship in contrast to God. Modern translators may do more harm than good when they translate Mammon as wealth, riches or money because this obscures the origin of the word.

Mammon was a term that came into the Hellenistic world from the Babylonians. The word carries with it the notion of trust and confidence. God wants us to place our confidence in Him (Proverbs 3:26). Faith can be defined as relying on the trustworthiness of God Almighty. Worshipping Mammon, by contrast, is having confidence in the material rather than the spiritual.

Placing our faith or confidence in Mammon instead of God is foolish for many reasons, but ultimately it comes down to lack of faith in God's ability to take care of us. Rather than trust Him, we trust the material and temporal realm. The love of money is the root of all sorts of evil according to scripture, but many people are devoted to it (I Timothy 6:10). Mammon or wealth is a much broader concept than Federal Reserve Notes under the mattress. Mammon encompasses all the features of our modern economic system upon which we depend to provide for us, everything from 401Ks to degrees from prestigious academic institutions, from stock portfolios to connections with the right people in our social network.

Humanity has a choice set before it. We can worship the King of the Nations presented by John, or we can worship the beast who enables us to buy and sell. Jesus said *No one can serve two masters because he will love one and despise the other.* Despise is a very strong word; it means to regard with contempt, distaste, disgust, or disdain, to scorn or loathe. We are caught in a dilemma, while we may not wish to despise God; we certainly do love wealth here in America. We want to say we love God while we love wealth, but this is impossible. A wise man once said the phrase 'in god we trust' was appropriately placed on Federal Reserve notes as this accurately identifies them as the god in whom we trust. With the recent economic events Americans are worried sick. Is our confidence placed in the world's economic system and the wisdom of the board of governors of the Federal Reserve Board? Or is our faith in the Creator God who governs the universe?

Jesus had financial advice for his first century followers. He said, *Do not lay up for yourselves treasures on earth, where moth and rust consume and thieves break in and steal* (Matthew 6:19). He told his disciples, *Watch out. Be on your guard against all kinds of greed; a man's life does not consist of the abundance of the things which he possesses* (Luke 12:15). All material treasures on earth are ultimately destined to perish and even if they did not, we are eventually separated from them by death. We cannot take them with us. Life is short. *What does it profit a man if he gains the whole world and loses his own soul?* (Mark 8:36).

The Mark that Facilitates Commerce

Anyone applying for a credit card or loan quickly learns the significance of a credit score in today's economy. The credit score determines whether a person gets a loan at all and dictates the interest rate at which money will be lent or credit extended. A credit score signifies a person's relative worth as a potential debtor. A statistical formula owned by a private corporation computes the probability that an individual will repay the debt. A high score indicates that it is quite likely the creditor will repay the debt, while a low score indicates the creditor is less likely to make payments on the debt in the upcoming 12 to 18 months. Credit scores are used to predict future behavior; as such they function as a prophetic device. Based on the computation reflected in a credit score, people are valued as consumers of credit, or debtors, and ranked as to their worth to lenders.

The multiple regression equation used to generate credit scores is proprietary which means it belongs to a private corporation and it is not subject to peer review.

In other words, the accuracy of the predictions is not open to review by impartial mathematicians. Neither the validity nor reliability of the mathematical models used to produce credit scores is open to scrutiny by reputable scientists. The margin of error associated with credit scores is not public either. This is perhaps the most serious objection to the widespread use of credit scores. An important part of the scientific process is the practice of peer review. When a scientist asserts a particular finding, he publishes his methods along with his results. Other scientists have access to this information so they can independently evaluate the truthfulness of the conclusions. The mathematical procedures for computing credit scores are not subject to scientific review. There is every reason to be skeptical about credit scores being predictive of a particular individual's future behavior.

Credit scores are fortune telling devices, they are intended to foretell what will happen in the economic realm to a consumer. Fortune telling is the practice of predicting information about a person's life. A poor score is a negative omen, forecasting economic difficulties. Some may object to this comparison because credit scores are based on data rather than tea leaves, but the point is that both are designed to predict the future.

Credit scores grew out of the practice of lenders sharing information among themselves about folks who borrowed money and never repaid it. Why lend money to someone who would not, or could not, repay? Why indeed? The bible offers a very different answer to this question than does the world.

> *One who is gracious to a poor man lends to the LORD, And He will repay him for his good deed* (Psalm 19:17). *On the other hand, he who oppresses the poor and needy…lends money on interest and takes increase, will he live? He will not live! He has committed all these abominations…* (Ezekiel 18:10-14).

Lending money to the poor at interest is an abomination from God's perspective. Again, from God's perspective, only the poor need to borrow money. People are poor because they do not have money or resources. If you are not poor, it is because you have money and therefore never need to borrow any. Study those passages carefully for they reveal two motivations for lending money. Some lenders are motivated to be gracious to the poor and help them in their need. In this case, they are really lending to God because He says that He will repay such lenders for their kindness. When money is loaned under this system, no interest is to be charged. God guarantees the loan. Even if the poor person never repays what was borrowed, God Himself will make it good to the lender, one way or another.

Another kind of lending takes place when the lender sees desperate need and takes this as an opportunity to make a profit by charging interest on a loan. God considers this an abomination. Abomination conveys disgust; the visceral emotion when something turns our stomach because it is infectious, unclean, or otherwise offensive. Disgust makes us want to vomit. The practice of lending money to the poor at interest makes God sick. Notice in both cases, the lenders are giving money to the poor and needy who must borrow to meet the basic necessities of life.

For what reason do middle class Americans need to borrow? We are among the richest people on the planet. We make up less than ten percent of the world's population and control about 85 percent of the world's wealth. Right now the whole world's economy is in distress because of loans made to people who had no means to repay. But these loans were not to buy bread and milk for hungry children; these were loans for real estate and consumer goods rather than necessities. Greed it seems has plunged the economy of the world into crisis.

In the early days of our nation when common sense prevailed, loans were not made to people who had no means to repay. Such people were often recipients of charity, but it was considered foolishness to loan them money. Common sense has given way to greed and the current practice of charging people who have no means to repay higher and higher rates of interest because of their desperation. Where is the logic in charging 28 percent compound interest on a loan to a man who has no money? A poor man would have great difficulty repaying even the principal sum. Only a desperate soul would consider borrowing money at high rates of interest. Banks loan money to subprime borrowers because this group is more profitable than lending to people who do not need loans. Banks make about 70 percent of their revenue from subprime borrowers charging fees and higher interest rates. One bank is offering a credit card now with a whopping 79.9 percent interest rate. The card is being offered to the so-called subprime households, typically with credit scores below the range from 640 to 700. This outrageous interest rate has been justified by the bank's CEO in these words, "Even when the cost of credit is astronomical, for people in true emergencies, it's much better than not having access to credit." In a true emergency is it necessary for the poor among us to borrow money at 79.9 percent interest? No wonder God Almighty might be disgusted with us.

The bible gives instructions about lending money, and about borrowing money. In order to grasp the essential contrast between worshipping God and worshipping the beast, it is necessary to understand what the bible says about economics.

> *If you lend money to My people, to the poor among you, you are not to act as a creditor to him; you shall not charge him interest.* (Exodus 22:25)

> *If one of your countrymen becomes poor and is*

> *unable to support himself among you, help him*
> *as you would an alien or a temporary resident,*
> *so he can continue to live among you. Do not*
> *take interest of any kind from him, but fear your*
> *God, so that your countryman may continue to*
> *live among you. You must not lend him money*
> *at interest or sell him food at a profit.* (Lev.
> 25:35-37)

These passages are drawn from the Old Testament and reflect the laws of the nation of Israel when God was their King. In the book of Revelation, God's reign is extended and He is called by the title *King of the Nations.* There is no evidence that God has changed His fiscal policies over the ages. There is no evidence that He now condones what He once condemned. Apart from wishful thinking, there is no reason to believe God has changed His mind about economics.

Credit scores are used to establish interest rates for borrowers. Some households are being asked to pay 79.9 percent interest in order to have access to credit in the event of an emergency. Credit scores are now used for many reasons beyond loans. Utility companies, employers, landlords, and insurance companies use credit scores to make decisions about doing business with people. The value of men and women has been reduced to a numerical score calculated by a mathematical formula by a machine. In the eloquent language of the old King James translation:

> *through covetousness shall they with feigned*
> *words make merchandise of you: whose*
> *judgment now of a long time lingereth not, and*
> *their damnation slumbereth not..."* (II Peter
> 3:2)

Credit scores are the means corporations use to

communicate among themselves about consumers, human merchandise, human beings as a commodity. Perhaps you have never considered yourself as a commodity. A credit score reflects the relative value assigned to a human being treated as a commodity. One human being with a 640 credit score is the same as another human being with a 640 credit score when we are treated as a commodity. Credit scores are used to predict the behavior of groups of people averaged together. The business of predicting the future is very lucrative for corporations engaged in it. Three major credit reporting agencies in the United States maintain data files on people which are used to generate credit scores: Equifax, Experian, and TransUnion. These are the corporations that store the data which is the raw material used to produce a credit score.

Equifax is the oldest of the three, founded as Retail Credit Company in 1899. Today the company has records on about 400 million creditors around the globe. It makes about 1.5 billion dollars a year and has around 7000 employees. The following was taken from an article by Simson Garfinkel published in "Wired" in September 1995.

Columbia University Professor Alan Westin, who attacked Equifax for its cavalier attitude toward the accuracy of its information on consumers, and for giving out that information to practically anyone who asked for it. In a March 1970 edition of The New York Times, Westin argued that the Retail Credit files "may include 'facts, statistics, inaccuracies and rumors' ... about virtually every phase of a person's life; his marital troubles, jobs, school history, childhood, sex life, and political activities." Companies used such reports to avoid extending credit to people who were judged to be morally lacking. The theory was that if you beat your spouse or engaged in deviant sexual practices, you probably couldn't be trusted to pay back a loan. To make matters worse, consumers had no rights to see the information collected on them. Many didn't even know the files existed. In the same month, Westin attacked Retail Credit in congressional testimony. The hearings came at a pivotal time: Retail Credit was about to computerize its files. "Almost inevitably, transferring information from a manual file to a computer triggers a threat to civil liberties, to privacy, to a man's very humanity because access is so simple," argued Westin in the <u>Times</u>. The effect, he continued, is that it becomes harder and harder for people to escape from the mistakes of their past, or to move in search of a second chance. Those hearings resulted in the passage of the Fair Credit Reporting Act in October of that year, which gave consumers rights regarding information stored about them in corporate databanks. Some observers believe the hearings prompted Retail Credit to change its name to Equifax in 1975.

For most of its existence, Equifax sold information to businesses. The company currently makes additional revenue by charging people to assume responsibility for the accuracy of the information in Equifax's data files. People are urged to monitor their credit reports for errors, but are required to pay money to do so, apart from one free report a year. This shifts the burden onto the consumer for correcting data files these companies keep about us. TransUnion purchased its first credit bureau in 1969. One plaintiff won $5.3 million dollars because it took TransUnion more than six years to correct errors. Experian, the third major player, has a chief executive who makes around 4 million dollars a year. Obviously this is a very profitable industry, keeping records on consumers and generating credit scores about them to sell to other businesses.

The interested reader will learn a great deal more about the credit reporting agencies by visiting corporate web pages for these companies rather than the web pages they have set up for consumers. Take time to do this and learn that TransUnion conducts studies on consumer behavior. It recently reported a trend for people to pay credit cards before mortgages. You will also find that TransUnion (and no doubt its competitors), "wants to help U.S. consumers get a better handle on how credit works, when they have access to it, and what their part is in that process. To do so, the company has introduced a credit education video series on its U.S. website entitled 'Understanding Your Credit.' The series features 5 topically-based segments, knowledge quizzes for each segment and informational links to related content at TransUnion.com. The videos can be accessed free of charge …"

A credit report is not a credit score. The credit report is based on the data file of information collected by these companies. The data often comes from other companies. Each of the three major credit reporting agencies will produce a slightly different credit score based on variations in data on file and the particular proprietary formula for logistic probability modeling it uses. This is why the same person might have three different credit score calculated to be 616, 656 or 666. The numbers differ because both the data and the equation differ somewhat. It would be strange to visit three different doctors on the same day be given three different heights, but this merely shows the difference between a fact like physical height and a credit score.

Your credit score was assigned to you, it was not something you asked for and you have little or no control over getting scored. The number belongs to the entity that assigned it to you. Credit reporting agencies calculate the number from information gleaned from many sources, and for a fee they sell this information and the score to other corporations. Credit scores are three digit numbers calculated and assigned to all, small and great, rich and poor, freemen and slave to facilitate commercial transactions in the modern economy. Credit scores have all the features necessary to serve as the mark of the beast described in the book of Revelation.

The Creation of the Mark

In the beginning, all of the three major credit bureaus, Experian, Equifax and TransUnion collaborated with Fair Isaac and Company (FICO) to establish the scoring method used to rate consumers. FICO was started in 1956 by engineer Bill Fair and mathematician Earl Isaac. The San Rafael, California Company transformed itself over the next several decades into the multinational Fair Isaac Corporation of modern times. FICO has diversified and currently analyzes ATM traffic at 11,000 banks, processes 90 percent of roaming cellular call records, manages 700 million credit card accounts around the world, and claims among its customers 70 percent of the top 50 insurance companies. FICO brags that it now services 2000 companies in 60 countries and is growing.

Explore Fair Isaac Corporation's home page on the Internet and learn more. For instance, the 100 billionth FICO Score was sold in 2007. This is truly a phenomenal number when you consider there are fewer than 7 billion people on the planet. It was achieved by reporting on those of us who have a credit score many, many times. FICO's success is evident from its customers, which include 9 of the top 10 Fortune 500 companies, over 90 of the top US banks, half of the top 50 US retailers, and 8 of the world's top 10 pharmaceutical companies. Clearly FICO is a major player in the world's economy. FICO's statistical models are used around the planet now, not just in North American and Europe. The FICO score is used in Russia, Turkey, Saudi Arabia, and Brazil, along with many other places. Recently FICO opened an office in Beijing, China, giving it another billion human beings to mark.

Thanks to the tremendous success of FICO, a credit score is now nearly essential for commercial transactions. It would be difficult at least, if not impossible to get a loan for a house or a car without having a credit score. Some companies will not even deliver fuel oil unless the recipient can furnish a score. We are not talking about having a poor score, but not having a score at all. As it is written,

> *And he causes all, the small and the great, and*
> *the rich and the poor, and the freemen and the*
> *slaves, to be given a mark on their right hand or*
> *on their forehead, and he provides that no one*
> *will be able to buy or to sell, except the one who*
> *has the mark. . .*

Americans tend to be ignorant of their credit scores and the workings of credit reporting agencies. This may be a dangerous ignorance. A 2003 survey by the Consumer Federation of American found that only 2 percent of Americans knew their actual credit score.

According to the Governors of the Federal Reserve, a credit score ranks consumers by the likelihood they will become seriously delinquent on accounts in the next 18 to 24 months. It is possible, indeed even probable, that being assigned a poor score hastens economic distress and makes it more likely a person will become delinquent. Think about what happens when creditors raise interest rates for an individual who was barely making ends meet. Monthly minimum payments rise as a credit score declines, but wages do not increase. Interest rates for loans and consumer credit are higher for individuals whose scores fall below the mid-600s. Ironically this happens to be the very range of numbers mentioned in variations of John's manuscripts as the mark the beast assigns to man, 616, 656 and 666.

The practice of credit scoring began in the late 1950s to support lending decisions by the credit departments of large retail stores and finance companies. Storing credit information about customers began even earlier. By the end of the 1970s most of the nation's largest commercial banks and credit card companies used credit scoring systems to evaluate new applicants for lines of credit. In the beginning it was complicated and rather expensive for a company to obtain an individual's credit history. Advances in technology in another decade made it possible for lenders to buy generic credit scores on people who were not their customers. As technology has improved, the cost of maintaining electronic records dropped dramatically. It is now feasible to collect and store data on millions of private citizens, data that can be sold for a profit.

There is a relevant moral distinction between an individual entering into a contract with a company and failing to honor the contract and a company buying information on private citizens who were never their customers. This distinction appears to be lost on corporations in their efforts to solicit for new customers. Over time, many new uses for credit scores have been devised and the mathematical models for generating the scores modified, enabling credit scores to be used beyond merely calculating the likelihood an individual would repay a debt. The current versions of these mathematical models can compute the profitability of lending money at a particular interest rate to a consumer representing a particular degree of risk. The programs for producing credit scores have turned people into commodities. The fourth amendment to the United States Constitution says, "*The right of the people to be secure in their persons, houses, papers, and effects, against unreasonable searches and seizures, shall not be violated, and no Warrants shall issue, but upon probable cause, supported by Oath or affirmation, and particularly describing the place to be searched, and the persons or things to be seized."* How has it come to pass that private companies are allowed to collect personal information on so many citizens? Why do corporations get to seize digital information on citizens?

The original sort of credit card still exists as a department store card which represents a line of credit with a particular merchant. The development of statistical models to evaluate credit risk has enabled large scale open-ended consumer lending. The first revolving consumer credit card was issued in 1958 by Bank of America. It was accepted by merchants across the state of California. In less than a decade, Bank of American arranged for banks outside the state of California to use its cards. Bank of America is a behemoth doing business in over 150 countries and with 99 percent of fortune 500 companies. As of 2010 it was the fifth largest company in the United States, one deemed too big to fail.

When did you give permission for private information about you to be stored by a for profit company to peddle? Read the fine print in the paperwork from the bank about its credit card and you are likely to see that you inadvertently gave consent to all this data sharing. The particular company you intended to conduct business with reserved the right to share information with its "family of business" which sounds warm and friendly. Businesses do not have families, but they are part of conglomerates and consortiums. One major wireless service provider told customers they had 45 days to 'opt out' of data sharing. The company intended to share data about calls made and received, billing information, and technical information with its affiliates, agents and parent companies. Credit reporting agencies could be considered affiliates of any company which conducts business with them. So now the twisted logic by which we inadvertently granted permission to have our privacy violated becomes evident.

Each national credit agency holds records on millions of people. Of course such massive records are likely to contain factual errors. Credit scores are not part of these static reports, but are computed using a mathematical program upon request. This keeps credit scores current. It also insures they will be based on any bad information stored in a file on a consumer that is not corrected. A clerical error can put someone else's defaulted loan into a credit file 15 minutes before a score is run to determine the interest rate on a car loan. The burden of discovering and correcting the error falls on the consumer, not on the company profiting from selling the data and scores. We should all be outraged at this treatment. Companies share information with each other about us, buy and selling it, and the burden of making it factual correct falls on us.

You waive your right to privacy simply by entering into a business relationship with any company that shares your personal data with any of the credit reporting agencies. We human beings do not get to ask credit reporting agencies to close our files, we are not their customers. All we are able to do is attempt to keep the information accurate. Of course, we can pay for protection from the same company that is putting us at risk, a service that is becoming profitable to the credit reporting agencies. There is another organization that charges for protection from the harm it might do but it is certainly not considered a legitimate business.

According to a report prepared for the United States Congress by the Federal Reserve Board of Governors, credit scores can be based on information that is not maintained in the credit report people are allowed to review and correct. In other words, you do not have access to the total information companies are sharing about you. The Board of Governors did not elaborate on the nature of this additional information. Given the fact that credit reporting agencies gather data from

30,000 or more sources, they can learn a great deal about each of us. In our digital age, the data in a credit file can include the title of magazines purchased at the local grocery store. Are you reading *National Enquirer, Good Housekeeping,* or *Fitness* magazine? Which one makes you the better credit risk? It is conceivable such data is weighed into the proprietary models for computing credit scores. Such trivial factors can become part of the record even if you pay cash if you use a store card at the register.

No law compels any creditor to report data to the credit agencies; they choose to do this voluntarily. Companies share your information because it benefits them. What would happen if consumers selected which companies to do business with based on how much privacy they afforded us? Corporations care about profits. Cutting into profits may be the only effective way to communicate with corporations,

Currently, about three out of four adults in the United States have data files with credit reporting agencies. Credit reporting agencies are working diligently to collect information on more of us, with the goal of having files on each and every one of us. The credit reporting agencies are creative in finding new sources of information about people. FICO has devised new models for subgroups of consumers who lack the traditional data used for computing a credit score. In other words, even if you have never borrowed money from a lender, the goal is to assign you a number. FICO developed the NextGen model for marking people who do not borrow money. FICOs NextGen model will be based on data collected from payments on utility bills, bank deposit records, and even regular payments for child care. Clearly FICO does not want anyone to escape its reach. "We will do whatever it takes to protect the reliability and accuracy of FICO credit scores for lenders, and to ensure lenders can continue to use FICO scores with confidence when making their most important customer decisions," according to Dr. Mark Greene, CEO of Fair Isaac. The loyalty of this corporation goes to the bankers, naturally.

While it makes some sense to evaluate past payment behavior before lending money, other uses of FICO scores have nothing to do with borrowing and repaying debts. Automobile insurance companies use credit scores to set rates for policies. Given the fact the insurance companies successfully lobbied to make car insurance mandatory, this can be quite harmful to the poor. An individual who drove for 30 years without ever filing a claim or being issued a moving violation is a good driver by any reasonable definition of words. In terms of potential risk, this driver should only pay the smallest of car insurance premiums. Now that the automobile insurance company uses credit scores to set rates, it can use a credit score to charge this excellent driver higher premiums. Actual driving behavior need not overcome a less than stellar credit score. People with lower credit scores do not cause more accidents, they simply file more claims. Perhaps because they cannot afford to pay out-of-pocket for car repairs they may naively think the purpose of paying premiums was to enable them to get the car repaired. The purpose of insurance premiums is to make money for car insurance companies; everything else is a cost of doing business.

The insurance companies can make any claims they want to make about relationships between credit scores and driving behavior, but these are unverifiable statistical assertions. No one has the data to challenge the industry. At best there may be a weak correlation between credit scores and driving behavior, but correlation never, ever proves causality. Even weak correlations become statistically significant when massive numbers of cases are used in computations. This is a truth that every undergraduate should learn from an introductory statistics course. If insurance companies crunch numbers involving millions of policies, a tiny, nearly zero correlation can achieve statistical significance and be used to justify this use of credit scores.

If the statistical models used by the companies included covariates like age and experience, how much predictive power is left in the model for credit scores? Younger, inexperienced drivers will also tend to have lower credit scores. Should they be penalized twice? Remember, human beings do not get to challenge any of these statistical models. The models are proprietary, which is another way of saying they are a black art. We only know they work because the companies which own them claim they work. Work for what? Increasing revenue? Do they work so well that past a certain credit score, say 750, we can know the driver will never be involved in an automobile accident? Is a perfect credit score a sign of a perfect driver? If it is, why should people with great credit scores have to pay car insurance premiums at all? Obviously the purpose of paying premiums is for insurance companies to make money. Car insurance companies get away with using credit scores by asserting that they have data that shows a correlation between credit scores and the likelihood an individual will file a claim. Are they willing to share this data and let independent statisticians examine it? Of course the companies are not willing to share their computational formulas. The Emperor has no clothes.

There is no statistical model that can predict the behavior of any particular individual in the future. Like divination, statistical modeling is a systematic method for organizing what appear to be disjointed, random facts to provide insight into a problem. Divination methods vary by culture. Being a highly technological culture, we like high speed computers and mathematical models.

All statistical modeling includes a margin of error. The insurance companies have discovered that using credit scores allows them to collect higher premiums from a greater number of people, thereby increasing profits. Of course the best predictor of future driving behavior is past driving behavior, not a score based on past financial behavior. Nearly every automobile insurance company, 92 out of 100, polled in a recent survey by Conning & Company and an increasing number of homeowners insurance companies use credit scores to set prices. What will be next? Can we anticipate health insurance companies using credit scores to establish premiums?

Maybe consumers need to seek out companies that will not make inappropriate use of credit scores, and consumers ought to be the judge of what constitutes inappropriateness. Perhaps companies would get the point if we stopped doing business with the worst offenders and sought out companies that weighed driving skills as relevant data for selling car insurance, for example. The trend of using credit scores to fix prices can be expected to expand to other products. The difference between a stellar credit score and a terrible one translates into the difference between obtaining a mortgage at 4 percent or 14 percent. What will happen to the poor among us when this differential is applied to every good and service? How will the poor survive?

At the present time, insurance companies are powerful lobbyists. They have managed to make various sorts of insurance mandatory. They have succeeded in making health insurance mandatory as well. At the present time about 1 in 5 dollars in the United States economy goes on health care. It is predicted that in the near future 1 out of 2 collars will go for health care. Can you see the future where all of your paycheck goes to insuring you against any possible risk?

The Beast Revealed

Assuming that credit scores are the mark of the beast that comes from the earth in the figurative speech of Revelation, we can identify the beast as the world's financial system. This beast is described as having two horns like a lamb, but it speaks like a dragon. The imagery suggests a false savior. Earlier John described the Lamb, looking as if it had been slain, standing in the center of the throne worthy of worship because He purchased people for God with his blood. The crowd surrounding the throne, consisting of men and angels sing, *"Worthy is the Lamb, who was slain, to receive power and wealth and wisdom and strength and honor and glory and praise!"*(Revelation 5:12). The contrast is between the 'Lamb who was slain' and the 'beast with two horns like a lamb' accords with the central theme of Revelation, the contrast between faith in God and faith in Mammon.

John says that the beast coming out of the earth speaks like a dragon. The identity of the dragon is disclosed in Revelation 12:9, *"The great dragon was hurled down-that ancient serpent called the devil, or Satan, who leads the whole world astray."* The scripture provides at least two other instances of Satan speaking. In perhaps one of the most ancient portions of scripture, we read, *"Does Job fear God for nothing?" Satan replied. "Have you not put a hedge around him and his household and everything he has? You have blessed the work of his hands, so that his flocks and herds are spread throughout the land. But stretch out your hand and strike everything he has, and he will surely curse you to your face."*(Job 1:9-11) Satan here challenges Job's motives for worshipping God, asserting that Job worships God for the sake of material prosperity and physical wellbeing. We hear from Satan again when he tempts Jesus. *The devil led him up to a high place and showed him in an instant all the kingdoms of the world. And he said to him, "I will give you all their authority and splendor, for it has been given to me, and I can give it to anyone I want to. So if you worship me, it will all be yours." Jesus answered, "It is written: 'Worship the Lord your God and serve him only.'"* (Luke 4:5-8).Some two thousand years had elapsed between these incidents, but what Satan says reveals his perspective on what is important, the material realm.

Why might it be appropriate to call the world's vast network of interlocking multinational corporations beastly? The term beast occurs often in the pages of scripture and it is always used in distinction to man. The fundamental difference between man and beast is the sort of life man possesses that beasts do not. This is the life which was breathed into mankind by the Creator and is discussed by theologians as the *imago dei*. The lofty concept of what it means to bear the image of God is beyond the scope of this book but it includes the mental faculties of human consciousness and conscience. Humans are privileged to have thoughts which alternately defend or accuse us depending on our actions, and this gives us the privilege of making moral choices. Beasts instinctively choose pleasure and avoid pain and can be conditioned to respond, but beasts lack the capacity to make reasoned moral choices. Expediency rather than morality governs the behavior of the beasts of the field. Men may of course choose to conduct themselves like beasts, leading a life governed by their appetites and thus behaving like dumb, unreasoning animals (II Peter 2:12).

Where did the global transnational financial system come from? Fifty of the wealthiest entities in the world are corporations rather than nation states. A corporation is a *legal personality* created to engage in the business of buying and selling. The defining feature of a corporation is its legal independence from flesh-and-blood beings created by God in His image. Human beings create corporations here on earth. For this reason it is fitting that the image in Revelation is a beast from the earth.

A British judge is famous for saying a corporation is, "a figment of the imagination, lacking both a body to be kicked and a soul to be damned." The judge seems to have been paraphrasing Lord Chancellor Thurlow who asked rhetorically, "did you ever expect a corporation to have a conscience, when it has no soul to be damned and no body to be kicked?" Lacking immortal souls, corporations cannot stand before the Almighty on the Day of Judgment to account for deeds done in the flesh. Of course if individual human beings chartered corporations to evade personal responsibility, they will face the judgment, as will each of us.

The peculiar thing about corporations, which have neither flesh nor soul, is that they enjoy the same rights as people have at this point in history. Corporations can buy and sell other corporations. It may be that corporations even have more rights than mere people. A corporation can get too big to fail, but people never get that big. Once chartered, a corporation exists perpetually. A great deal of evil in the world is perpetrated by corporations merely bent on achieving the prime directive for which they were created: maximizing profits for shareholders. The documentary film "The Corporation" reveals the sociopathic nature of the corporate beast and is worth watching.

We would all be better off if we have paid more attention to our American history lessons in high school. The Boston tea party was as much a rebellion against the British East India

Company as it was against the British crown. Commerce in Boston was shut down by the British government until the colonists paid the East India Company for the tea that went into the harbor. Colonists responded with more protests and then convened the First Continental Congress. The colonists were none too keen on the British government giving the East India Company a monopoly on tea. The British East India Company was a corporation and the forerunner of modern multinationals.

Our forefathers had a certain animosity towards corporations which echoes in the declaration, "We hold these truths to be self-evident, that all men are endowed by their Creator with certain inalienable rights, among these the right to life, liberty and the pursuit of happiness." The founding fathers were intent on preserving the liberty of flesh and blood human beings as inalienable rights. The liberty we Americans take for granted is held much dearer when human beings are traded like things. It is shameful that slavery still exists on earth today. The miracle we call America was created by men and women who wanted a nation free from corporate slavery. It took a bloody civil war to accomplish their dream, but it was finally achieved, at least for a time.

The early citizens of the United States were wary of corporations for good reason, and kept the beast on a short leash. The provision in the constitution for voters to be landowners should be understood as a defense against the mercantile powers that made laws for dealing with each other on the high seas and across national boundaries. Mercantile law, the law of merchants, is a system of rules and regulations used by traders to resolve conflicts with other traders. It is mercantile law that it allows creditors to transfer debts between themselves—which is ultimately a way of transferring debtors as well. This feature of mercantile law dates back in time at least to ancient Babylon.

The status of corporations in the United States changed in

1819 when the Supreme Court ruled that corporate charters were inviolable and beyond the reach of government. The decision in that case set a precedent and started a trend. The next major case on corporations came before the court in 1886, *Santa Clara County v. Southern Pacific Railroad*. This case is interpreted as giving corporations the status of persons under law, persons entitled to all the same rights as the freed slaves under the 14th amendment. In legal proceedings, flesh and blood human beings are often referred to as natural persons to distinguish them from non-natural or artificial persons, corporations. In jurisprudence the category of natural persons is further subdivided into free persons and slaves. Freemen are natural persons who have preserved their natural liberty and therefore enjoy the right to do anything which is not specifically prohibited by law. Slaves do not enjoy natural liberty as they are in the power of their owners being property. Sometimes under law, slaves are treated as natural persons, but many times they are treated merely as things. Debt capitalism can and often does tend to reduce freemen to the status of slaves.

Corporations are beasts because they are incapable of moral reasoning, they lack the capacity. Stockholders and employees of corporations are natural persons and quite capable of moral reasoning, unless they destroy their consciences by hardening their hearts. Corporations as artificial persons do not possess consciences: they are mandated to obey a corporate charter in the same way a dumb beast follows its instincts. From another perspective, corporations are similar to cancer cells. Cancer cells do not intend to hurt anyone because cancer cells are incapable of intentions of any sort, good or evil. Once called into existence, a corporation has no choice but serve its charter which is most likely a directive to maximize profits for shareholders. Even corporate social responsibility efforts serve this function, maximizing profits for shareholders. Corporations are socially responsible as long as social responsibility is a means to maximize profits.

Having considered the nature of corporations, let us return to the beast that arises out of the earth described in Revelation. A class of corporations called central banks control the monetary system of the world. In the United States, a private corporation known as the Federal Reserve System is responsible for the money used in our banking system, Federal Reserve Notes. The Federal Reserve System was created in a special session of the Senate by an act that passed at 11:45 p.m. on December 24, 1913. As the Federal Reserve is a private for-profit corporation, perhaps we ought to wonder about who owns it? According to one book about the Federal Reserve, seven of its top ten stock holders live in foreign countries. In his 1987 book, "Secrets of the Temple: How the Federal Reserve Runs the Country" William Grieder explains how the Federal Reserve Board works. He says, *"Above all, money was a function of faith. It required implicit and universal social consent that was indeed mysterious. To create money and use it, each one must believe, and everyone must believe. Only then did worthless pieces of paper take on value."*

There was a point in time when a bank note was a receipt for something of value held by a bank. The bank note could be used to redeem that item. Once the dollar was taken off the gold standard, money truly became an illusion. Now a bank note is simply a piece of paper worth what we believe about it, or it may be even less tangible, merely a figure blinking on a computer screen.

A Hierarchy of Beasts

In 2005, the British Broadcasting Corporation ran a program called "Who Run's Your World" on which experts debated whether global corporations are the most powerful beasts in the jungle. Multinationals are a special category of corporations, which operate across national boundaries. To maximize profits, multinationals seek the least expensive nations for production and the most lucrative markets for selling. This explains call centers in India where college graduates make $300-400 a month working in an electronic sweat shop. The American who once answered the call might not be working at all.

Multinationals are the driving force for the globalization of world commerce. The magnitude of their collective force is evident if one considers that 51 of the world's largest economies are corporations rather than nations. The combined income of the top 200 corporations on earth exceeds the combined income of the poorest 25 percent of all human beings. Multinational employ less than one percent of earth's people.

The World Trade Organization (WTO) may be more powerful than any other entity on earth. The organization promotes open borders for business and commerce. WTO supports a global patent law known as the Trade Related Intellectual Property Rights Agreement (TRIP). We consider this particular instrument for illustration purposes; it is certainly not the only agreement worth learning considering. Among its many applications, TRIP protects pharmaceutical corporations. More than 1200 drugs came to market in the two decades between 1975 and 1995, fewer than 20 targeted tropical diseases. In contrast, half the top 30 money making drugs in the United States for treat depression or anxiety. Given the sickness and suffering of the people who inhabit the tropical regions of earth, why so few drugs to treat their many and real afflictions? The world's poor cannot afford expensive new drugs, so they are not a good market. Pharmaceutical companies make money by selling drugs to people with money, not to sick ones. Several excellent books discuss the pharmaceutical industry in detail, including 'Selling Sickness.'

Americans are the world's primary consumers of everything. We are people with money to purchase products from pharmaceutical corporations, so their products are designed to be sold to us. From the perspective of corporate charters producing drugs for wealthy people makes more sense than producing drugs for sick people. It also makes sense for pharmaceutical companies to find new ways to persuade the wealthiest people in the world to believe they are suffering various ailments and in need of ever increasing numbers of pharmaceutical products. These products are now advertised directly to us on television so we will be able to ask our doctors what to prescribe for us by name. Mandatory insurance that covers the cost of all these drugs is liable to become too expensive for all of us. One pharmaceutical corporation recently obtained patent rights to a drug that has been used for decades to prevent premature delivery and it raised the cost a thousand fold.

How can we reason logically about the cost of pharmaceuticals? RSV is a virus many children get before their second birthday. Out of 200 infants and toddlers who are exposed, between one and four will be hospitalized on account of it. Premature infants are at the highest risk for infection with this virus and are the most likely to be hospitalized. There is a drug that reduces the odds an infant will be hospitalized with RSV. The price of treating one preemie for six months is about $10,000. Treatment reduces the odds of hospitalization from 1 in 25 to 1 in 100 which means 26 infants need to be treated for six months at a cost of over $300,000 to keep one baby from being hospitalized. As children grow they need larger more expensive doses of the drug, so it could cost two or three million dollars to prevent one hospitalization. Drug cost needs to be understood from the perspective of how many people have to be treated for how long at what price to save one person from what risk? Vaccinations that confer years of immunity to frequently fatal illnesses are a bargain from this perspective.

What does this have to do with the World Trade Organization and TRIP? Patents are a kind of license granted by a government to an inventor to protect an idea from rivals, in court if necessary. Patents prevent rivals from profiting from an invention or idea without the permission of the patent holder. A patent is treated like property in that it can be bought or sold. Under the TRIP agreement nearly every nation on earth has adopted similar patent regulations, notable exceptions being India and Brazil. These nations decided they could not afford to be a part of trade agreements on drugs. No company in any nation which signed the agreement can manufacture drugs for its citizens and sell them inexpensively without permission from the patent holder. This is true even when there is no chance poverty stricken customers can afford to purchase drugs from the company that holds a patent. Even if the pharmaceutical corporation which holds the patent is not producing the drug, no other company can produce it without permission until the patent expires. Sometimes giant pharmaceutical companies make drugs for these poor markets, but this is generally because of tax benefits for doing so that improve the bottom line.

We live in the age of astonishing biomedical advances. Along with these incredible advances comes the fact that human genes have been patented by corporations. In the United States over three million gene patents have been filed by corporations. To understand consider the case of a man whose spleen was removed at a medical center affiliated with a university. The doctor who treated him was involved in a research project subsidized by tax dollars. The doctor established a cell line from the man's T-lymphocytes. A company purchased the patent rights to the cell line. A court ruled the man had no property rights to his cells, to the DNA contained within his cells, or to any profits made from the use of his cells. Michael Crichton used this case as the basis for one of his novels. Perhaps the author of DNA objects to corporations infringing on His intellectual property rights.

We have passively permitted the evolution and growth of a global financial system where corporations can legally buy and sell us, or at least parts of us, including bits of the human genetic code. Is it acceptable for corporations to hold intellectual property rights over parts of the human genome? Are we just parts for sale, one type of commodity among many others? If you find this troubling, consider a statement made by the president of Rigel Pharmaceutical Corporation, "It seems to be okay to patent every animal in the zoo but us [humans], a reflection of our need to believe that we are special– not part of the continuum of nature."

An Unchecked Beast

The most important thing to understand about a credit score is that it belongs to the corporate entities that use it to mark people. We have no real control over our score. The bankers who loan money manipulate credit scores and raise them to increase interest rates at will by dropping limits on lines of credit. Lenders do not need consent to drop credit lines and thereby lower credit scores. A credit score has less to do with human behavior than it has to do with the needs of banks and multinational corporations at a given point in time.

The FICO model is used to compute credit scores. It is based heavily on a factor called "credit utilization ratio." This is the portion of available credit that is used at a point in time. For example, an individual with $1,000 charged on each of five different credit cards, each with a $5,000 limit has a credit utilization ratio of 20 percent. Another individual who charged $5,000 on his only credit card with its $5,000 credit limit has a utilization ratio of 100 percent. Although both individuals are in debt for the same amount of money, the person with five credit cards has a lower utilization ratio and thus, all things being equal, a better credit score. The credit card companies can arbitrarily drop credit limits on cards and even close cards. Banks have been doing this to consumers across the country over the past several years. The individual who had five credit cards suddenly discovered he had five maxed out credit cards. This change in his credit utilization ratio damages his credit score. In response to the lower credit score, credit card companies raised interest rates on cards. The essential point is that the change in his credit score had nothing to do with this person's behavior; it was rather the result of unilateral activity on the part of the lenders. What one card company decides to do can cause a domino effect, a bank drops a limit on a line of credit, the person's credit score goes down, another bank raises interest rates on a card, and other card companies now follow suit. The person's credit utilization ratio goes up, his credit score plummets. Because of the perceived risk of the poorer score, the individual is charged higher interest rates on existing accounts. If the consumer doesn't like the new interest rates, his only recourse is to close the accounts, but this also has a negative impact on his credit score. The consumer also faces the real possibility of having difficulty finding a better rate elsewhere because of his lower credit score.

The tactical plan seems to call for getting consumers hooked on credit cards by offering them incentives, such as the "would you like ten percent off today's purchases?" Or "zero interest for six months?" Once the consumer has several credit cards with small sums charged on each card, drop limits and raise the interest rates. When the letter comes notifying the consumer of the higher interest rate on the card, his only recourse is to close the account, further harming his credit score.

While many consumers have been hooked on credit because we live in an instant gratification society, some relied on credit to meet real emergencies, the transmission on the car had to be repaired or medical bills had to be paid. No matter the reason for the debt in the first place, with the economy in recession, households are facing declining income. With the economic crunch, overtime and part time work has been harder to find. At the same time, taxes, utilities and food prices continue to rise. Under such circumstances, consumers may well wonder why bank card companies can charge 29 percent interest or more on old debts while the bank only pays one percent on a person's savings account. Isn't it the money in savings accounts that is being loaned out?

In the face of these difficult economic times, how are lenders getting consumers to pay up? Watch television and see the advertisements for the terrible fates which befall people with poor credit scores. People get bonked on the head when they pop up from holes in the ground, or drive junky cars and use antiquated cell phones if they have bad credit scores. From annoying pop up ads on internet web sites to clever television spots, media messages are targeting consumers to make us to care deeply about our mark. Clearly these are designed to make us fear having a bad credit score.

The economic mess our nation faces today was caused by greed, *greed which amounts to idolatry* according to the bible. We borrowed money to buy things we didn't need. Consumers spent with little concern for the consequences because shopping made us happy. We thought if we bought a sufficient amount of the right material goods we would achieve happiness. Long ago the philosopher Aristotle said that happiness is a moral state, not a psychological one, but we missed that lesson. This is not a message played during prime time commercials that saturate the public airwaves. As long as we paid interest to the bankers, the economy chugged along. Psychologists, marketing consultants and behavioral economists worked diligently to manipulate consumers into purchasing products. People behaved like the corporations wanted us to behave; we sat in front of commercial television and were programmed to consume. Like rats in a Skinner box, we pressed the lever, working for reinforcements, things to fill the void left in our psyche-a void created by Madison Avenue to get us to spend.

A consumer is a commodity without an individual

identity except as it is expressed in a decision to purchase a product or service from the perspective of a corporation. People once reacted to prices in a rational manner. If the price went up, people bought less of the product because they could not afford to buy more and live within their means. If many people stopped buying the product, the lower demand would eventually bring down its price. The concept of 'supply and demand' undergirds much of what we assumed was true about our economic system. Unlike the old fashioned customer, the modern consumer shows greater neural activation on a brain scan after tasting wine from a bottle said to cost $90 than after tasting wine from a bottle said to cost $10. Perception has nothing to do with the actual taste of the wine because investigators poured the samples out of the same bottle. Similar studies have been done with tap water. Years of programming have conditioned us to believe that it must be better if it costs more. Multibillion dollar media campaigns have targeted us, and increasingly our children, to get us to spend money we don't have on things we don't even need.

A new economic system has been created by applying the best behavioral science to the study of economic behavior. Corporations invest billions of dollars collecting data on human behavior in order to control it. Data is collected from every possible source imaginable that might be used to get us to purchase another widget. From internet shopping habits to purchases at the local grocery store or Wal-Mart, it is being studied by experts to craft a marketing campaign. In a land where privacy is highly valued, this massive invasion of personal privacy is accepted in the name of commerce and pursuit of the almighty dollar. Commerce seems to be the only realm held sacred in modern America. The current global economic crisis is due to subjecting ourselves to marketing ploys that made us greedier and greedier. Much of our frenzy to accumulate material goods was paid for on credit or treating home equity like an ATM. Multinational corporations are inherently greedy; their corporate charters compel them to maximize profits by reducing the cost of production and increasing sales. Manipulating human beings to buy products is simply a cost of doing business.

These same corporate giants persuaded the government of the United States to give them billions and billions of dollars. Even the United States government does not have that kind of money sitting around in a back room in Washington DC. The government gets money by taking from its citizens, by printing it and thereby inflating the money supply and causing inflation, or by borrowing money. When people ask a bank for a sizeable loan, the bank uses an asset such as a house or car for collateral. In the event you fail to make the payments on the loan, the bank seizes the asset. When a nation goes to borrow money, where do they go and what do they offer for collateral? When the United States borrows billions of dollars from communist China, collateral is the government's ability to tax its citizens. Our future earnings are the collateral on the loans being taken out by the government when it goes trillions of dollars into debt. Your labor, the labor of your children, and the labor of your children's children will be used to pay back these loans. The final price tag for the bail-outs may be as much as $23 trillion dollars according to the Congressional Research Service.

Twenty-three trillion dollars is so much money it is difficult to even begin to imagine what it means. The sum is greater than all the money spent on all the wars the United States has ever fought (in today's dollars). If you spent a million dollars each day from the birth of Jesus Christ until now, you would not have spent even the first trillion of these dollars. This new $23 billion dollar debt is an addition to another $66 trillion dollars already owed for Medicare and Social Security. These are debts because the government spent the money earmarked for these programs. Take a look at your pay stub and realize that the money paid for Social Security and Medicare that is withheld from your check for your old age has already been spent. No wonder so many senior citizens are enraged by the present course of events. They have paid money all their lives into this system, and now the terms of the contract are about to be changed on them just when they need the money. Was Social Security a scam from its inception?

The bailout will increase the supply of money in circulation and this will lead to inflation. Inflation is an increase in the supply of money which causes more dollars to circulate and drives up prices. Consumer prices will rise along with taxes to pay the interest payments on the debts incurred by the government. Worst hit by the rising prices in our global economy will be the world's poor. Not the poor folks living in the trailer park across the tracks or in the projects in American's inner cities, the poor around the world who are struggling to get by on less than $2.50 a day. These people are already so poor that many of them are forced to send their children away to lives of bondage so they may eat rather than starve to death immediately. We live in a global economy, so what happens economically in the United States has repercussion for everyone on earth. The *King of the Nations* cares deeply about the plight of the poor who are invisible to us, He hears their cries.

The economic situation is so bad the United States is at risk of losing its excellent credit rating. The UN is considering finding a currency other than the dollar to serve as the world's standard. If our national credit rating goes down, taxpayers will be forced to pay higher interest rates on the national debt, at the same time we are paying higher interest rates on personal debts.

We weren't always a nation addicted to credit. Thirty years ago, few people had a credit card. Back in those days credit cards came with fixed interest rates and balances were paid off at the end of every month. If something unfortunate happened and it was not completely paid off, people lost sleep worrying about how they would get it paid off. Thirty years ago people did not use plastic at the grocery store or for other consumable goods. Times have changed and most major credit cards have variable interest rates, another concept which is an abomination in scripture as are other fluctuating weights and measures in commerce. When the Federal Reserve raises the interest rate it charges to its best customers, the big banks, they raise interest rates to consumers. But if the Federal Reserve lowers interest rates, banks charge any rate mentioned in the fine print mailed out with the card, or perhaps after the card was mailed out as a fine print amendment.

Storing all the digital information about millions of consumers in computers has led to yet another risk we face, the theft of our digital identities. Millions of credit-card account numbers are compromised each year. There is little or nothing any individual can do to force a company to maintain adequate cyber-security. Should your identity be in the data base that gets hacked, someone may have your name and social security number. They can then sell your identity or they can use it to borrow money or purchase goods. This creates a burden, an enormous one, for the person whose identity is stolen. It becomes that individual's responsibility to prove he wasn't the person who took out the loan or made the purchases. Corporations are now in the business of selling consumers protection against identity theft. Of course this protection comes from corporations who put your social security number in cyberspace for the hackers to find in the first place. Now corporations are willing and eager to sell another product, a product to protect us from their gross negligence.

The next time someone asks for your social security number, pause before you hand it over. Question why it is needed; ask how it will be used, how the company guarantees it cannot be stolen, how you will be compensated if it is, and what will happen if you refuse to give them the number. If you don't like these answers, do not share your social security number.

The company may refuse to do business with individuals who will not divulge social security numbers. Perhaps it would be prudent to take your business elsewhere and do business with a company that does not demand your social security number for identification. Do not give out a social security number just to facilitate record keeping for businesses. There are 8 million victims of identity theft each year in the US, people whose economic lives have been stolen. Eight million people who must, at great effort and cost to themselves, repair an assault made possible because they trusted corporate America.

Lessons from Babylon

Babylon is mentioned a number of times in the book of Revelation. What was so remarkable about this ancient empire that it was still relevant centuries later when John penned his prophecy? Surely one of the most graphic images in the entire book is that of a prostitute riding on a beast. On her forehead is written *"BABYLON THE GREAT, THE MOTHER OF HARLOTS AND OF THE ABOMINATIONS OF THE EARTH."* (Revelation 17:5)

One of the chief deities of the ancient Babylonians was the goddess Ishtar. In art she was often depicted as a naked woman; and literature described her as insatiable and unfaithful. If a picture paints a thousand words, what message should we get from this image of the harlot called Babylon riding on the beast? The Babylonian prostitute is said to be the mother of earthly abominations, but what does this mean? The central meaning conveyed must have to do with the fact prostitutes sell themselves.

The father of history, Herodotus (485-425 BC) reported that every woman in Babylon was compelled to offer service as a prostitute at Ishtar's temple at least once in her lifetime before she was eligible for marriage. Earnings from this temple transaction were given as an offering to the goddess Ishtar.

While scholars doubt the historical accuracy of this tale, it had been widely circulated by the time of John whose first readers would have heard this about the ancient Babylonians. Contrast this practice with the law for the nation of Israel under which wages from prostitution could not be offered to the LORD. Such wages were an abomination to Him (Deuteronomy 23:18). The daughters of Israel were not to profane themselves by engaging in prostitution. Matthew Henry notes in his commentary on the passage, "*We cannot honor God with our substance, unless it be honestly and honorably come by. It must not only be considered what we give, but how we got it. Where the borrower gets, or hopes to get, it is just that the lender should share the gain; but to him that borrows for necessary food, pity must be showed.*"

Not long after entering the promised land in the era of the judges, the Israelites are accused of playing the harlot having "*made Baal-berith their god*" (Judges 8:33). This theme is repeated throughout the history of the nation. Whenever the Israelites followed other gods, practicing wickedness in the process, God charged His people with harlotry. The Babylonians were an economic power in the ancient world for 1200 years until the 6th century before Christ. They were major players on the world stage during most of the era described in the pages of the Old Testament. When Nebuchadnezzar conquered Judah, taking captives and valuables from the temple from Israel to Babylon, among the captives was Daniel (II Chron.36:18). Daniel is the author of an important prophetic book in the Old Testament in which he describes a series of human empires as beasts. Although empires are a form of government, it is important to understand these were financially motivated endeavors, or it would be easy to miss a point of major relevance. Many scholars, including Isaac Newton, regard the book of Daniel as a key for deciphering the book of Revelation. The fate of the prostitute named Babylon is described in Revelation, and here we learn something about her destruction.

> *The merchants of the earth will weep and mourn over her because no one buys their cargoes any more—cargoes of gold, silver, precious stones and pearls; fine linen, purple, silk and scarlet cloth; every sort of citron wood, and articles of every kind made of ivory, costly wood, bronze, iron and marble; cargoes of cinnamon and spice, of incense, myrrh and frankincense, of wine and olive oil, of fine flour and wheat; cattle and sheep; horses and carriages; and bodies and souls of men.*(Revelation 18:11-12)

When luxury goods are no longer purchased the multinationals will weep. John was not writing about an empire gone for six centuries when he penned this prophecy. His image likely alludes to practices that originated with the ancient Babylonians.

Scholar G.C. Lee at Johns Hopkins University wrote a work entitled "Historical Jurisprudence" published in 1922. In it he writes, "The law of Babylonia has had an immense effect upon that of nearly all the countries of Europe . . . The complex Babylonian civilization, which produced a commercial law in advance of any other ancient system . . . The Babylonian Law developed to the fullest extent the idea of a Contract. Almost any possible business transaction was reduced to the form of a contract and was executed with the same formalities - i.e., with witnesses, notary, and signature. Thus the points as to deeds, sales, mortgages, loans, and banking are in no respect different in form from the matter of hiring, rent and leases, partnership, testaments, and domestic relations, including adoption. Transactions so very different could be reduced to the same principle, or brought under the one head, only by a highly abstract conception of contract itself."

Many concepts used in commercial transactions today originated with the ancient Babylonians. They were a people who took contracts seriously; swearing oaths before temple priests who served as the first notaries. Presumably the oaths carried the metaphysical sanction of the local deity. Of great significance to this discussion is the fact that Babylon is the first civilization known to history where merchants traded debts as a form of property. People could be reduced to slavery in Babylon if they could not meet their obligations under a contract; hence Babylonian merchants literally traded in the "souls of men." Through debt, human being were reduced to the status of cattle and regarded merely as things or commodities.

Slavery was common across the ancient world. Slaves produced goods and provided most of the labor for agricultural production. Slaves could be obtained from foreign wars; but many were reduced to slavery because of incurring debts they had no means to repay. Jesus used this all too familiar situation in his days to teach his listeners lessons about mercy. Today we tend to overlook the financial aspects of forgiveness, as if we have no material obligation to God.

Slave owners made money by hiring out slaves in order to profit from their labor. Babylon also included a class of free men who worked alongside slaves but earned higher wages. These freemen managed to be economically competitive because they bore their own health care costs while owners were liable for medical costs for slaves. This distinction remains with us in the modern economy as the difference between independent contractors and employees. There may be a profound lesson from ancient Babylon for us moderns. Is it better to earn higher wages and take responsibility for our own medical bills, or to expect others to cover the cost of our health care? Even before health care reform passed, coverage for a family of four ran an average of $13,000 a year. For a working family, this could easily represent a substantial raise. If one pays for one's medical care out of one's own pocket, one has a greater reason to be concerned about living a healthy lifestyle. If the cost of medical care is shifted to others, there is little incentive for staying physically fit. In fact, being physically unable to work might even appeal to those with mundane and difficult jobs.

The merchants of Babylon traded throughout the known world of the day. They organized gilds and created firms that survived over generations. Babylonians used precious metals as a medium of exchange. Money was initially loaned on the condition the borrower would repay the loan by labor, but this practice gave way in time to loans at high interest rates. The Babylonian government collected taxes and customs on imported goods. An important aspect of all Babylonian commerce was the written contract. If a dispute arose, parties to a contract selected an arbitrator to hear the case. Reading records from ancient Babylon led one author to remark, they *"reveal to us a people greedy of gain, exacting, litigious, and almost exclusively absorbed by material concerns"* (Dawn of Civilization, p. 760).

John writes about the fate of the prostitute called Babylon in Revelation 18:2-5.

> *Fallen, fallen is Babylon the great! She has become a dwelling place of demons and a prison of every unclean spirit, and a prison of every unclean and hateful bird. For all the nations have drunk of the wine of the passion of her immorality, and the kings of the earth have committed acts of immorality with her, and the merchants of the earth have become rich by the wealth of her sensuality. I heard another voice from heaven, saying, "Come out of her, my people, so that you will not participate in*

> *her sins and receive of her plagues; for her sins*
> *have piled up as high as heaven, and God has*
> *remembered her iniquities."*

Unless God's people want to share in the catastrophe that befalls Babylon, they are warned from heaven to "*Come out of her*" rather than participate in her sins and receive her plagues. What sins? Gold offered for sale at the local department store, the chocolate and sugar in the candy bar at the local movie house may all be tainted by the suffering of exploited child slaves. In prostitution, the most intimate human relationship becomes a financial transaction. Prostitutes sell themselves for money; but this Babylonian whore sells herself for luxury goods. This is a graphic image of our present condition.

James, the half-brother of Jesus, offered advice to the rich at the end of time:

> *Come now, you rich, weep and howl for your*
> *miseries which are coming upon you. Your riches*
> *have rotted and your garments have become*
> *moth-eaten. Your gold and silver have rusted;*
> *and their rust will be a witness against you and*
> *consume your flesh like fire. It is in the last days*
> *that you have stored up your treasure. Behold,*
> *the pay of the laborers who mowed your fields,*
> *and which has been withheld by you, cries out*
> *against you, and the outcry of those who did the*
> *harvesting has reached the Lord of the Sabbath.*
> *You have lived luxuriously on the earth and led*
> *a life of wanton pleasure; you have fattened your*
> *hearts in a day of slaughter.* (James 5:1-5)

Gold and silver rust at about 410° F: a temperature incompatible with biological life. This is the fate of those who live a luxurious life of wanton pleasure with no regard for the cries of the workers who bring in the harvest. Americans are among the world's wealthiest people. You may not see yourself as rich, but if you store your food in a refrigerator, sleep in a bed, and put your clothes in a closet, you are among the richest 15 percent of humans on the planet. If you cannot see this, it is because you do not consider your economic circumstances alongside the two billion people on the planet struggling to live on $2.50 a day.

According to the United Nations Children Fund (UNICEF), over 200,000 children work as slaves in West and Central Africa. Although child slavery is considered illegal in the Ivory Coast, the government there says the practice continues because foreign multinational corporations want cheap cocoa beans. To produce a crop at a price that allows them to make at least a little profit to support their own families, owners of cocoa farms use child labor. The cries of these children along with those of others around the globe reach the ears of the Lord of the Harvest. Rather than be oblivious to the truth, we need to consider carefully how our purchases are produced. If our only concern is getting an item for the lowest possible price we may be contributing to the suffering of innocent children. We can afford to pay $3 or $4 for a bar of chocolate so the laborers who work the fields make a living wage; we are among the 15 percent of the wealthiest people on earth. Exploiting the poor in sweat shops, on plantations and in mines for the sake of luxury goods is immoral. Looking the other way so we do not see it puts us in the company of the rich man who never noticed Lazarus at his gate, or the religious leaders who passed by the man who had been beaten and left for dead alongside a certain road.

Commentators on the book of Revelation have interpreted the harlot as the Roman Catholic Church. It is historical fact the Roman Church gave European princes vast sections of the planet to plunder. This did contribute to the concentration of wealth in Europe at the expense of people in colonies. The exploitation of the world's poor continues, but now it is done in the name of goods for wealthy consumers.

An Insatiable Beast

Rolling Stone magazine ran an article by Matt Taibbi explaining how the current global economic crisis came to pass. It was not about money according to Taibbi, it was about grabbing power. In his words:

> *"It's time to admit it: We're fools, protagonists in a kind of gruesome comedy about the marriage of greed and stupidity. And the worst part about it is that we're still in denial — we still think this is some kind of unfortunate accident, not something that was created by the group of psychopaths on Wall Street whom we allowed to gang-rape the American Dream."*

His article details how the financial crisis was triggered by a power grab by a small group of very wealthy people who used packages of debts or collateralized debt obligations (CDO). A CDO might include credit card debt, car loans and house mortgages. It might even include another bundle of debt. This concept of packaging debts is a sophisticated form of gambling based on the probability some debtors will pay off their obligations, even if some others in the package don't.

Using this strategy, banks sold CDOs containing very risky loans to institutional investors who were once very conservative in their investment practices. These investors managed pension funds and such. Bankers made fortunes selling CDOs after persuading the corporations that rank banks there was almost no chance the combination of debtors in a CDO would all default. Unlike conventional loans CDOs were evaluated by mathematical models rather than the assets by which the loans were secured. The world's economic crisis was caused by a group of men who thought they could predict the future using mathematical models. The CDO was smoke and mirrors, a statistical illusion.

Bankers got greedy and in the process they plunged the world's economy into free fall. The government has regulations that require banks to keep a fraction of money they loan on reserve in the event someone comes into the bank and wants their money. Bankers found a clever way around regulations by promising to bail each other out in the event of any trouble with the CDOs. In the process of making arrangements to bail each other out, the financial institutions created products that were so complicated even bank regulators could not follow the paper trails. In particular, two corporate giants, Bank of American and Citigroup, crushed the competition by trading IOUs with each other as if they were 'real money.' Given the nature of Federal Reserve Notes perhaps this is not too surprising. When the banks could not bail themselves out, they turned to the government.

Today there is no country in the world that uses the gold standard. Previously until 1971 the United States dollar was backed by gold. Before that it was the British pound. Right now, the US dollar serves as the reference currency for the world. Once in addition to the dollar, the pound, the frank, the mark and the yen served in this capacity. International agreements settled on the dollar because of its stability and the vastness of the United States economy. When the government bailed out the corporations that were too big to a fail, it means we bailed them out. The stockholders for the corporations were the beneficiaries of that bailout. How much did it cost us to help them out?

Most Americans have no concept of large numbers. David Schwartz, author of the children's book, "How much is a million" provides useful tangible examples for us. One million seconds comes in about 11½ days. A billion seconds is 32 years. Does that help clarify the difference between a million and a billion? Now how do you feel about your government giving the bankers 700 billion dollars? Bloomberg says the stimulus package cost at least $8.5 trillion dollars. A trillion seconds is 32,000 years. Assuming an estimated U.S population of 305 million, your personal share of the bailout comes to $28,000 or so. The real cost is likely to be much greater.

Escaping Babylon

Come out of Babylon and participation in a financial system built on greed and stupidity. Biblically speaking, repentance is a change of mind, it is an intellectual decision. Seventy-two percent of Americans report feeling stressed out over money. A few are so stressed out they resort to murdering a spouse and their children and then commit suicide. Pollsters say 77 percent of Americans claim allegiance to some form of Christianity. Considering that 72 percent of Americans are stressed over money, it is clear that many who claim to follow Christ are living in Babylon. Being stressed out about finances is a symptom of placing faith in Mammon rather than God, and that is sin. The stress is a symptom that we expect money to provide for us, which reveals the object of our faith is misplaced. One does not need to be in debt to be worshipping Mammon.

The *borrower is slave to the lender* is no more a command than is the assertion by Jesus that the *poor will always be with us*. These are factual statements and warnings for us to heed from the pages of scripture. If you have been a participant in the world's economic system, buying and selling, and borrowing to do so, you are likely in debt.

If you want out of the mess you are in financially and

spiritually, you must begin by making an intellectual decision to walk away. Getting out of Babylon requires repentance.

Repentance is both very difficult and very easy. It is difficult because of our pride. Repentance means owning up to sin. It means admitting our cares and financial anxieties might reflect a moral issue; certainly being anxious about money reflects a moral issue. The excellent news is that repentance provides immediate relief and offers a solution to money troubles. Whatever the form or complexity of financial issues we think we face, the real problem is putting confidence in Mammon instead of God. Repentance is changing our mind and our allegiance. No matter what our material circumstances, we can learn to be content, just like the Apostle Paul wrote:

> *I have **learned to be content** in whatever circumstances I am. **I know how to get along with humble means**, and I also know how to live in prosperity; in any and every circumstance **I have learned the secret** of being filled and going hungry, both of having abundance and suffering need*(Philippians 4:10-12).

Being content in our circumstances is a learned behavior, and this is a very great truth. We can learn how to be content no matter what our circumstances.

The first major lesson we need to learn to escape Babylon is to live in reality. First and foremost, **do not spend money you do not have**. This is a simple truth, but we humans tend to struggle with simple truths. We do not know what tomorrow will bring, so we should not spend tomorrow's money today. Each day has troubles enough of its own. The model prayer Jesus taught us is *give us this day our daily bread* (Matthew 6:11). Not "give us this day our daily bread for the next two weeks, two months, or two years." Contentment means learning to live in the financial present. We may neither borrow from the future, nor wish the past was different. Each day has troubles enough of its own.

Living with reality means having a budget, and there are many excellent resources that can be helpful from books to websites. A simple but effective approach begins with disposable income, the real amount that comes home. The ink on the pay stub which indicates gross salary is something of an illusion. If you generally get a large tax refund at the end of every year, you ought to change withholdings rather than loan money at no interest to the government. Money that comes in, whether it is a tax refund or social security one day ought to be treated as disposable income at that point in time. Disposable income is what is left after taxes and other mandatory withholdings are taken. Earmark ten percent of disposable income for each of three categories: saving, giving and debt liquidation. These sums must come out before developing your budget for spending. After considering factors presented in subsequent chapters you might decide to adjust the amount set aside for debt liquidation in order to escape from Babylon sooner.

The median family income in the United States is about $50,000. If we assume a married couple with 2 dependents making this much a year, their monthly income would be $3660 after federal income tax, social security and Medicare. State taxes reduce disposable income still further and in New York; they would be in a 6.85 percent tax bracket and pay another $285 a month in state taxes. The family would have a disposable income of $3375. If they earmark $337 for savings, $337 for giving and $337 for debt liquidation, they would have $2365 to live on. One reason many Americans are in such economic distress is because we fail to understand the simple economic difference between gross income and what is really available to spend

What is the most prudent way for a family to allocate this money? Perhaps we would do well to be content if we have food, drink and clothing (Matthew 6:25-34). The first category in the budget ought to be for nutritious food to sustain biological life. The United States Department of Agriculture publishes the cost of food at home, which ranges from $583 on a thrifty food plan for a family of four up to $1152 for a liberal plan. If you make less than the median US income of $50,000 a year for your family, use the thrifty food plan. If you make more than the median income, the first category worthy of allocating additional funds to would be food. According to the USDA, an adult female spends between $150 and $300 and an adult male slightly more, $168 to $332. Whether you have more or less than the median US income, divide your bread with the poor and spend $40 a month of the food budget on feeding the hungry elsewhere in the world and God will graciously reward your kindness. This budget provides an individual with $4 to $9 a day for food, certainly not enough to eat out often. Prudent shopping would however provide wholesome healthy food to be prepared at home, food made by God, not corporations. Clean drinking water is available from the tap for most Americans, so beverage expenses can be confined to tea, coffee and an occasional bottle of wine. Not purchasing beverages other than these will reduce costs and improve health. Eating nutritiously is essential to human biology; it is an investment in health. Hygiene is also a necessity of life. The budget needs to allocate funds to pay for soap, laundry, shampoo and toothpaste. Many people in the developing world die for lack of these basic necessities. Sleep is also a biological necessity. The need for shelter might be an apartment or mortgage on a house, but it is wise to remember that our biological for sleep could be met with an air mattress in the corner of a room. A reasonable starting figure for shelter is 30-34 percent of disposable income and this needs to include utilities such as heat, lights, and garbage. It does not include cable television or air conditioning as these are not biological necessities. In order to live a life of contentment, we need to distinguish between biological needs and desires that fulfill needs which are not biological.

The next category for consideration is budgeting for health and safety needs. It includes basic cell phone service to communicate with the work place and to call for help in an emergency. It is possible to have two telephones for the adults in the family for less than $20 a month on a prepaid family plan. The first phone gets 50 minutes a month for $9.99 and the second phone gets 40 minutes for $5.00. Choose the right phone initially and you get double minutes for life. The essential need to communicate can be met without signing contracts for the latest, greatest new technology. This category also includes funds to pay for health care, which may include your share of insurance provided by an employer, premium co-pays or deductibles. If you cannot afford health insurance, definitely set aside $100 a month for medical expenses. Regular exercise is crucial to staying healthy and most regions of the country offer basic health club memberships for as little as $10 a month for an adult. Allocate money for this expense and then make good use of it. This category addresses needs related to holding a job, namely clothing and a means of getting to work. Being presentable at work can be achieved by shopping carefully for quality used clothing and caring for it. It is not a need to purchase a new wardrobe each season. Americans could take lessons from Europeans in this area. Holding a job includes having a reliable means of transportation to get to work. This need can be met by riding the bus or a bicycle, carpooling or walking. If none of these is feasible for your circumstances, understand that having a reliable used car fulfills the need. The latest, greatest model might not be a need. If it fulfills esteem needs it belongs in another category. Americans tend to take it for granted that we should own a car, but cars are expensive. The cost of operating a car includes insurance, license and registration fees, and depreciation, along with operating costs such as fuel, maintenance, and tires. Purchasing a car also includes the cost of finance charges. The experts suggest that you not spend more than 20 percent of your disposable income on a car but that is probably too much for meeting the basic need. Try allocating only 10 percent of disposable income on transportation.

After budgeting for the biological necessities of life, security and job expenses, money can be allocated to meeting psychological needs. We humans have a need for affiliation, we need our friends and we need to enjoy good times together. This is the category that includes additional phone minutes for text messaging and stamps for sending cards and letters. This category also allocates funds for a high speed internet connection for the household. This makes it possible to use Skype to talk to family members out of town, to access a wealth of information, and even watch films. Consult the Old Testament law and you will find that it was obligatory to set aside funds to travel to attend celebrations, so budget 3 percent of disposable income for vacations, travel and entertainment.

Other human needs for self-esteem, self-actualization and peak experiences are best met by giving your time and substance to others. Money cannot buy happiness, but giving it away does make us happier. As you go through this budgeting process, you may find that these categories and priorities are quite a bit different from what you are currently spending – and that might just be the problem if you are anxious about finances.

Here is a sample budget for a family of four living on a gross income of $50,000 a year. It applies the categories and priorities outlined above. Take the time to figure out what your budget would look like if you adopted this approach. What would you need to change to be content with your circumstances and live within your means?

Sample Budget for Median Income Family of Four	
Disposable Income	$3375
10 percent savings	337
10 percent giving	337
10 percent debt liquidation	337
Balance for living expenses	**2364**
Biological Necessities -1837	
Food 600 Water from tap	0
Hygiene	30
Shelter (30-34 percent disposable)	1147
Health and Safety –416	
Basic phone	20
Health care	100
Health club membership	20
Clothing necessary for work	40
Basic transportation	236
Psychological Needs -110	
Communication with friends	10
Information	30
Vacations/Recreation/Entertainment	70

In order to live within your means, most likely you have to stop buying things that are not needs. You need food, you need water, and you need to sleep. These necessities are promoted in advertising. Be aware it will take considerable effort to get Babylon's siren songs out of mind. We have all been programmed by corporations and bankers who make money on interest charged for providing immediate gratification. We have been charged for borrowing from our futures and spending it today, but the future is not guaranteed. It will make the task of repenting considerably easier without the seductive songs from Babylon playing in the background. Turn off all devices that bring messages to spend money. Turn off televisions with its commercials. Stop channeling the Prince of Power of the airwaves into your home and mind. Corporations invest millions of dollars formulating messages to get us to spend money we don't have on products we don't need. Maybe you think you are not affected by advertisements, but you would be wrong in that belief. Scientists who conduct brain imaging studies have discovered that the same brain regions activated by religious thoughts are activated by images presented in ads. Tremendous effort has gone into making consumers feel this way about products.

If you are affluent and have money left after this budget is created, should you spend it on sensual pleasures and share the harlot's fate? Or might it be wiser to find a way to invest at least a portion of it in the Kingdom of Heaven?

To find favor with God, it is necessary to bring forth fruit in keeping with repentance. Just talking the talk will not suffice; one must also walk the walk. Begin by sitting down with pen and paper to figure out how much money is available each month, then live on less than that amount. Begin with the decision to live on less money than you bring home. Be realistic as you plan; only count the money you can depend upon. Borrowing money at compound interest from bankers insures that you will never be free of Babylon. Worse, you will be participating in her sins. We need to be content with our circumstances. Living within our means is the first step to contentment. Freedom starts with a decision. Since most of us can't control how much we earn, we must control what we spend.

Most Americans are already in consumer debt and some are sinking. The second step to getting out of Babylon is buying freedom. You want to be free of owing the bankers for consumer debts; you want none of your wages going in compound interest for consumer goods to make banks richer. In the days of the Old Testament, Israelites sometimes had to sell their labor as indentured servants for a period of years to pay off debts. You might need to embrace this model for setting yourself free. There really is no choice, you either work for your freedom or you die a slave to consumer debt. A slave has no choice about laboring day after day for someone else's profit. If you owe someone else money, repay it following biblical principles. You are not obligated to follow worldly principles regarding debts once you repent of life in Babylon. Liberty is sweet and far to be preferred over a life of indentured service for corporations. The bible says we should be in *debt to no man and owe no man anything except love* (Romans 13:8).

Having decided to live on less than disposable income and setting a goal to achieve economic freedom, what's next? Eliminating consumer debts is an essential step towards leaving Babylon. It will require intellectual effort to formulate a workable plan and it may take several years of discipline to work the plan. The first step out of Babylon is taken the day you refuse to borrow any more money from bankers. Having made that decision, your next task involves serious study as you research your state's laws that apply to debts. Begin by tallying up the total amount of money owe to everyone for everything. Debts fall into several categories. Some are secured by tangible objects such as a home or a car. You might be able to achieve immediate relief from these debts by giving back the home or car. Most likely you owe more on the asset than it is worth, so in reality these debts are also secured by your labor. After prayerfully considering your situation, you may decide that you ought to stay in your house or car. Assuming you make sufficient money to afford your mortgage and car payment, pay these bills first. If you don't the asset can be taken and you may still owe money. Another category of debts are sums owed to friends and relatives. Pay these back in full or ask to have them reduced or forgiven. If they forgive your debts, you are obligated to forgive others their debts too. The third category of debt you owe is unsecured consumer debt. Never miss a mortgage or car payment to make credit card payments. Do not get behind on utility bills to make credit card payments either. Review the budget suggestions made above. If the mortgage and utilities are taking more than 34 percent of disposable income, or if the car is taking more than 10 percent, you may be over spent. You should be able to pay the car off in two years. If you cannot pay it off in this timeframe, you might not be able to afford it.

Financial freedom means developing a plan for paying off all consumer debt in a reasonable time. Tally up the total debt and divide it by 60 months (five years) if you make the median income or less. Can you pay off your total consumer debt (not counting your car and mortgage) in five years using just 10 percent of your take home income? Could you do it if you allocated 15 percent of disposable income? Could you do it in three years? What is the least amount of time in which you can reasonably pay off your debts without borrowing any more money? To avoid borrowing more money it is imperative that you set aside money, you must have savings. You must have savings. As you plan, set aside the same amount for savings that you allocate to paying off old debts. If you pay ten percent on old debts and save ten percent, can pay off your debts in five years?

For many readers, the minimum payments creditors expect exceeds what you can afford to pay and meet expenses for savings, giving, and essentials. If you find yourself in such circumstances, do not despair. After you repent, you will begin to reap a better crop than the one sown in Babylon in due time. Investigate state laws regarding wage garnishment because these form the basis for formulating a plan for getting out of debt.

Each state has fixed a maximum portion of wages that can be taken by creditors if they go to the trouble to get a judgment. In many states this is 10 percent of gross income. If this sum is all a court with jurisdiction will allow creditors to take after a judgment this is all you need to give them each month. Once you repent of serving Mammon, you are not obligated to give Caesar or those chartered by Caesar more than what is due them according to Caesar. The amount you need to pay each month to your creditors is a function of the law in the state where you live. You have no moral obligation to go beyond obedience to the letter of the law in repaying debts. Read this statement again: you have no moral obligation to go beyond obedience to the letter of the law in paying back debts. *Render unto Caesar that which is Caesar's and unto God that which is God's.* God has clearly spelled out our obligations to give to those in need, to support our households, and to honor Him. We do not honor God by neglecting these obligations in order to pay creditors more than the law requires. Corporations are creatures of the state and what is due to them is a function of law.

No matter how deeply in debt you may be, creditors cannot take more of your wages than the portion specified by your state's law in any given month. You are allowed to keep most of what you earn to provide for yourself and your dependents. For families who have been paying creditors 20, 30 or 40 percent of monthly income, this should be sweet relief. Their burden can be lifted. At the same time you investigate the laws that pertain to your situation, find out whether there is a maximum period of time in which you must pay off creditors under an agreement. You need to be fully informed before you negotiate with your creditors to arrive at a plan to pay off your consumer debts. You need facts at your command before you enter into this discussion.

In New York, if someone's gross income is $60,000 a year, 10 percent of that could be garnished. This amounts to $500 a month. In five years, this person could pay a total of $30,000, including interest and principle. This sum is the total amount that all creditors could collectively take in a state that allows 10 percent of wages to be garnished. Some states do not allow wages to be taken for debts other than for child support, alimony, school loans, or taxes.

For a family struggling to make minimum payments on credit card debts, this is a very important concept to understand. Knowledge is power. Visit the credit card calculator site at www.federalreserve.gov and find out what happens to the person who just makes minimum payments on credit cards at compound interest rates. Consider the family that only has $8000 charged at 17 percent interest and makes just the minimum payment of $160 each month. It will take 37 years for them to pay off this balance if they do not incur any additional charges on the card. They will pay $17,752 interest in that period of time. If they paid $500 a month on the card, it would be paid off in 19 months even at 17 percent interest. In this case, the interest would have come to just $1,137.

If you owe large sums on high interest credit cards, you cannot afford to make minimum payments because you will never get out of debt. You will spend your life as an economic slave in Babylon. It would be much better to have the creditor get a judgment in a court because the compound interest would become simple interest at a lower rate. Depending on the state where you live, creditors have 3 to 20 years to collect on a judgment and are allowed to collect 6 to 20 percent simple interest. Interest rates for judgments are typically substantially lower than the compound rates charged by credit card companies. Take this to heart, most in debt Americans would be better off economically if their credit card debts were turned into judgments because of the usury interest rates being charged by lenders.

The point of learning about wage garnishments, statutes of limitations for debt collection, and interest rates is to equip you to be wise about managing finances. Once you leave Babylon, you will give up borrowing money at compound interest rates to purchase consumer goods. It will be essential to have money saved to meet emergencies and to take advantage of actual sales on items you need to purchase eventually. Families need money to live on, as well as money to save. It is imperative to live less than disposable income to save money at the same time debts are liquidated. For many Americans who are merely managing to pay the monthly minimum on credit card debts it will be impossible to get out of Babylon without making a drastic mid-course correction.

Credit cards are considered open lines of credit until you close them. If you want to negotiate payoff plans with credit card companies, you may need to close accounts. This will have a negative impact on your credit score. Leaving Babylon is going to have a negative impact on your credit score, embrace that truth. A "good credit score" means you are a valuable debtor. Do you want to be a debtor? If you have a good credit score it simply means you are willing and able to pay thousands of dollars in interest over the course of your lifetime to banks. Are you?

Wages cannot be garnished until a creditor goes to court and obtains a judgment. If you are not giving a creditor the amount they want each month, typically the minimum payment, the collections office might call you or the company might sell your debt to a collection agency. This is not a legal judgment; this is merely an attempt to collect the debt. Do not feel that you have to give these bill collectors more money than they would be entitled to as a matter of law, and that is the amount a court would give them in a judicial proceeding. The entire group of creditors is entitled to some fixed percent of your wages and you can calculate this sum. Individually, each of them is then entitled to some portion of that amount. You have no moral obligation to give them more than the law specifies. Creditors who go to court and get judgments only get to collect simple interest. Banks circumvented traditional usury laws in states by getting federal legislation passed that enabled them to ignore state usury limits. But when the banks seek judgments they have to comply with state laws and the usury limits become applicable. Usury, according to the USLegal's website, "is a civil or criminal violation involving charging more than the maximum interest rate allowed by law. The rate of interest legally allowed is governed by state statutes. If a court finds that the rate of interest on a loan is usurious, the interest due becomes void and only the principal of the loan needs to be repaid."

Knowing that your collective creditors only get a specified portion of your income allows you to create a plan for getting out of Babylon by living on a budget and being content. As long as you faithfully pay as much to your creditors as they are entitled to as a matter of law, they lack a good reason to take you to court. Creditors resort to court if they cannot get money by other means. It costs money to go to court to get a judgment. Some creditors may decide to take you to court, but understanding how garnishment works should reduce fear. It may be to your advantaged to have a debt reduced to a judgment at a simple interest rate. Voluntarily pay as much of your wages to creditors as they would obtain in a legal proceeding and live in peace. It will make little difference in your life if a creditor takes you to court except for the effect it may have on your credit score. The credit score should not matter after you realize what it is.

Beware of companies offering to settle or refinance debts. Many are unscrupulous, will make a great deal of money from your suffering, and will not do anything you cannot do for yourself. Before you consider one of these companies, ask yourself why are they offering this service? Obviously they are in the business of making money and will make money off your misery if you let them handle your financial affairs. Most charge fees and a percent of the total debt you owe. They pay themselves before they pay your creditors and they do not guarantee you will not be taken to court. Do you really need this kind of help? Once you figure out how the legal system works regarding debt, you can negotiate with your creditors. Non-profit consumer credit counseling services may be able to help you manage a plan to get out of debt.

Tragically, many Americans used home equity to refinance consumer debt. As the price of real estate has fallen, people have watched their homes become worth less than they owe on mortgages. If you are in this situation, realize you are not alone in having trouble making ends meet. Adjustable rate mortgages are increasing at the same time property values are dropping. This makes it impossible for some to refinance their mortgage at a lower interest rate or to take out a home equity loan to repair a leaking roof. Meanwhile, finance charges and fees are increasing on credit cards, consumer prices are creeping up along with taxes. Some families find it is impossible to escape their distress by selling the house to get out from under a mortgage they cannot afford. Families, who fully intended to be responsible when they borrowed, are struggling because of economic factors beyond their control.

The mistake we made in America was borrowing against the future. Heavily indebted, near bankrupt households need to negotiate with creditors to get some of their debt forgiven. Yes, forgiven. This forgiveness should be an incentive to be responsible about paying part of the debt in good faith. Assuming you want out of Babylon and are currently in debt to bankers, attempt to work out arrangements to buy your freedom.

If you are making minimum payments and not saving money, you have no cash in reserve in case of an emergency. Your only option in an emergency is more debt. This is debt bondage and it is not an acceptable way to live in contentment. Under these circumstances, it might be necessary to skip payments to credit card companies for a few months in order to build up an emergency fund. This will get the attention of the card company which may be more likely to negotiate with you. This will hurt your credit score of course, but it is more important to have real money saved for emergencies than the ability to take on more debt. You need your credit card account to be moved to a department where someone is authorized to negotiate terms on your account. As long as you are paying the minimum monthly $240 at 19% interest on a card with a $12,000 balance you are a valued consumer. The bank will be happy to accept this $240 for the rest of your life. You are a valued consumer because the bank will collect nearly $43,000 in interest from you for the next 58 years. The bank has no incentive to change its relationship with you. Why would it? The bank doesn't care if you are stressed out over trying to make ends meet. The bank doesn't care if you are feeding your children off the dollar menu at McDonalds in order to make the monthly payment. They corporation is profiting from the current arrangement. You want to change your relationship with it and be enrolled in the company's hardship program if it has one. To get into it, you have to demonstrate you cannot continue making payments. The clearest way to demonstrate this is by not making payments. After you get the bank's attention, let it know you want to close your account and pay off the account in two years at $500 a month (or whatever 10 percent of your disposable income happens to be.) Explain that you are not willing to pay any more in interest than the bank would get from a court after it got a judgment. Begin by asking the bank to just pay back the principal at zero percent interest

Before you start negotiating with your creditors, consider your circumstances in detail. What would happen if all your creditors were awarded judgments against you tomorrow morning? If you had to pay off your entire unsecured debt load over five years at 9 percent simple interest per year using 10 percent of your gross income, how much of your debt could you pay off? Sit down and calculate this sum. If you owe more than this amount you need to negotiate. Ask to pay zero percent interest or ask for a portion of the debt to be forgiven. It is unfortunate you may have to intentionally fall behind on your payments to make creditors willing to negotiate new terms. If you had a complete accounting of how much money you already paid over the years, you might realize that banks are not doing you a great favor by finally allowing you to pay back the principal. In many cases, the company has already been paid two or three times what was borrowed if you only made minimum payments.

Remember while you make your plan, the person on the other end of the telephone sees your consumer credit records. He knows how much you owe your creditors and the monthly payments you've been making. What he doesn't know is how much money you make each month. Maybe you need to share this information so he will understand the math. Explain if your circumstances have changed since you went into debt. Explain that you have come to the realization that you can no longer just pay interest for the rest of your working life. Explain you want out of debt. The person you are talking to doesn't really care about the struggles you are going through, but they do care about getting as much money as they can. Be honest while remembering the percent of your wages that can be taken. Each creditor is only entitled to its fair share although each creditor will consider itself to be privileged.

You absolutely need to have some money saved when you start this journey out of Babylon. You will need to close open credit cards and lines of credit to pay back principle sums. You aren't going to have those credit cards for emergencies. It the car needs tires; you will need to pay for them with cash. You need to have savings to rely on. You simply cannot continue borrowing money and ever be free of Babylon. Personal responsibility is crucial to your freedom.

It might be possible for you to keep one credit card with a local credit union if you pay it off monthly. Realize you may have to accept a high interest rate to have a credit card and a low credit limit. Your credit score is going to be poor once you turn your back on Babylon. Deal with any credit card by keeping it paid off. In fact, you might even want to preload it with money for emergencies if you have a card that allows this. It doesn't matter what the interest rate is on the card if you do not carry a balance on the card. The bank might want to charge you a fee for having a card if you never pay interest. Consider opening an account at a second financial institution and using a debit card on that account as your primary "credit card." Use it to access your emergency savings and charge yourself 12 percent compound interest for using it. Another possibility is getting a secured card or use PayPal for internet purchases.

If you cannot afford the stress of living in debt, you have to take action. It might be possible for you to negotiate with a creditor without being late on your payments, so try. However, creditors are more likely to negotiate after you are late. This might seem strange until you look at it from the corporate perspective. From its perspective if you have been paying, you can afford to continue paying. No matter how great a customer you have been over the years, the company only really cares about the next payment from you. Your goal is to pay off all unsecured debts in five years or less. You might be able to accomplish this if you can get your interest rate reduced and do not pay late fees or over limit fees. Does 10 percent of your gross income over the next five years pay off your debts? You need to have a goal in mind when you negotiate, and freedom is the goal.

Your home is another matter because you need to live somewhere. The question you need to consider when it comes to your home is whether you are living within your means. There are calculators on the web that will estimate how much house you can afford on a particular income. Ideally, your total monthly obligations including your mortgage should not exceed 36% of your monthly income according to the experts. If your house itself is taking twice this, you have a problem and might need to give up the house. Another strategy for keeping a home is getting more people contributing to the mortgage payments, taxes and upkeep. You will want to prayerfully consider your options. Having some legal claim to the roof over your head might be an advantage if the economy gets worse. Hold on to your home if you can and it seems wise. It may be that members of your extended family or friends will need a place to shelter. You also want to consider how much equity you currently have in your home as you plan your exit strategy. Do you know what your home is worth now after the housing bubble has popped? Do you have any equity left in your home? Should your property tax bill be reduced to reflect the new value of your home? Anyone who begins a serious effort to get out of debt needs to know their net worth and consider using assets to settle debts.

Planning Your Escape Route

In order to escape from Babylon, you need a plan for getting free of debt. Calculate your total consumer debt, including your car payment(s). The car loan is secured against the vehicle but it is very easy to owe more on a car than the vehicle is worth, so that negative equity becomes just another consumer debt. Given the current rate at which you are making payments can you pay off all your unsecured debt in five years? Are you giving your creditors what they would get by garnishing wages in your state? If not, consider living on less so you can be free sooner. Your goal is complete freedom from economic slavery.

What if you are so deeply in debt that you cannot dig yourself out in five years? State laws do not demand that you live on less than some specified portion of your wages. We are to render to Caesar the things that are Caesar's and to God the things that our God's. Federal Reserve Notes fall under Caesar's jurisdiction and it is acceptable to follow Caesar's rules for managing consumer debt. If you in debt so deeply that you cannot pay off your creditors in three to five years using 10 to 15 percent of your disposable income, the fault lies both with you and the institutions that loaned you money without any tangible security. No one owes corporations more than state laws permit them to collect.

It is not prudent to give creditors more than 10 to 15 percent of your disposable income for old consumer debts because this nearly guarantees you will fall deeper into debt over time since it is quite likely you will not be able to save any money. Consider the individual who makes $30,000 a year in New York. After paying social security, Medicare, federal and state taxes, he brings home about 70 percent of his gross, or a disposable income of $21,000. Assuming he needs 30 to 34 percent of that for shelter expense, he only has $900 to $1000 left to meet all other expenses. If he needs to finance and operate a used car, it could cost $400 a month. By living economically, he might be able to pay $175 a month to old debts while setting aside $175 a month in savings; but, he will have to subsist on $150 to $250 for everything else, including food, medical expenses, basic cell phone service, and work clothing. If his minimum payments are more than $175 each month it would be extremely difficult for him save any money.

A person struggling along under these circumstances is unlikely to be giving money to anyone else either. On average, Americans contribution just $1620 a year and given a median household income of about $50,000 a year in this country, we are giving less in tithes, offerings and charity than we ought. Many Americans are sending money paying interest on consumer debts that would be better spent on helping others in need. As a nation and as individuals, we need to repent of covetousness and greed which amounts to idolatry. Christians are admonished to make it our ambition to work in order to have to give to those in need (Ephesians 4:28). We are the richest people on earth and planet and we should help those struggling to live on $2.50 a day.

Is the moral obligation to pay off creditors more important than saving money for times of need or giving money to the poor? Judgments about the morality of human behavior need to be made in light of the scriptures rather than traditions passed down from Babylon. If you borrowed money because you were not content with your circumstances, lack of contentment was the sin. Repent by changing your mind and behavior. The lack of contentment, not the debt, is the sin. Owing money is not a sin; it is a source of vulnerability. Perhaps you are in debt because of medical bills or another personal economic disaster. Good people have bad things happen to them. Faith in God does not exempt us from the troubles that befall mankind. Study the book of *Job* to learn this truth. If you are in debt, you must correct the situation as soon as possible. Negotiate with your creditors and pay back as much as you can afford to without sliding further into debt.

It is likely many readers have been making payments on consumer debts over a number of years. If you have only been making minimum payments, you might be astonished how much money your creditors have already made because of compound interest. Most likely your creditors have already earned a handsome profit on your account. If they recover the principal sum or a sizeable portion of it they should be pleased. Leaving Babylon means you have no intention of being a valued customer for lenders. Lenders value customers who are willing to pay and pay and pay over a lifetime. Your goal is to get out of debt as soon as possible and not to give them any more of your wages. Your goal is to stop working as a debt slave to the beast. As soon as you adopt this mindset, you will be at odds with the corporate goal of profiting on your debt. The corporation wants you in economic slavery, laboring away to make its stockholders ricer. You want freedom.

Begin the process of getting your freedom by notifying creditors you are no longer one of their valued consumers by closing accounts. Credit card companies make fortunes on yearly fees, interest payments, penalties and late fees charged to customers for providing them with a line of credit. If you keep the credit account open, you agree to these terms and you make yourself vulnerable. You pay dearly for the privilege of being a valued customer. Change the relationship with the corporation if you do not want to be a commodity, a valued customer, whose treatment is dictated by a credit score. You want to be regarded as a human being with obligations to satisfy. Close lines of credit and pay off as much debt as you can in five years or less, but remember that you have to be saving money at the same time.

Your goal is achieving economic freedom. Free men do not owe their labor to corporations. Remember the goal during the process of negotiation with creditors. The total sum you are obliged to give creditors from wages is fixed by law. In many states this is a fixed percent of disposable wages. If lenders allowed you to go further into debt than this on unsecured loans they were greedy and irresponsible. No doubt they were looking to make money from late fees and penalties. They were fiscally irresponsible to loan more than you could afford to pay. Curiously, income is not a part of the data used to calculate credit scores. This displays a blatant disregard for state laws for recovering debts through wage garnishment, don't you think? Please remember, you may have been greedy, foolish or desperate when you got into debt, but the lenders are professionals. They had a fiduciary duty to act prudently. The greater fault is theirs.

Preparing yourself to negotiate with creditors will take time. You need to collect information and compute figures. You need to tally up the total sum you owe on all your unsecured debts, including those to relatives and friends. While you are making these calculations, you also need to know the percent each individual debt is of the entire sum. Consider the following example which lists debts from six accounts, totaling $35,000 on six accounts.

Creditor	Amount	Percent
Nan's Clothing	$ 5,000	14%
Capitalism One	10,000	29%
Capitalism Two	12,000	34%
Too many shoes Store	500	2%
Bank of Amber	2,500	7%
American Excess	5,000	14%
TOTAL	$35,000	100%

Each debt represents a percent of the total and this will help you decide how much to pay each creditor on a monthly basis. If for instance, the person would pay $375 a month if his wages were garnished in the state where he lives, he would give 34 percent of the $375, or $127.50 to Capitalism Two. American Excess would get 14 percent, or $52.50. After working up these figures, the debtor would write each creditor a letter and explain the sum that would be paid each month for the next five years to settle the account.

How will the creditors respond? If Bank of Excess expects the debtor to make a minimum payment of $100 a month for 22 years on the account, which is the minimum payment at 14% interest on a debt of $5,000. In that time, the Bank of Excess would make $6,110 in interest. The creditor's offer of $52.50 a month for the next five years is less than it wants. In theory, a person might be able to pay off this one debt in five years by increasing his minimum payment to $117 a month. The problem is our creditor probably cannot afford to pay each creditor enough money every month to pay off this debt with compound interest in five years. The creditor would need to make payments of $1034 each month to get this debt paid off in five years. He could afford to do this if he was grossing $177,257 a year.

Creditor	Amount	Pay off in 5 years	Interest Rate
Nan's Clothing	$ 5,000	112	12%
Capitalism One	10,000	317	29%
Capitalism Two	12,000	418	34%
Too many shoes Store	500	20	2%
Bank of Amber	2,500	50	7%
American Excess	5,000	117	14%
TOTAL	$35,000	1034	100%

What about people nearer the median income, what can they do? They can ask creditors for a debt restructuring plan. Companies use debt restructuring on outstanding debts to avoid defaulting on debts or in order to pay lower interest rates on debts. Companies restructure debt for each other by altering terms and provisions of existing debt and it is just business to them. Fictitious persons get to restructure debts and natural people should be able to restructure their debts as well. If our debtor can afford to pay back $375 a month, in five years he can pay back $22,500 of the principle sum. Yes, this is less than he owes at this point in time, but he has already been making payments on the original sums, perhaps for years.

How can you approach asking corporations to restructure consumer debt? Be polite when contacting each corporation's representative. You will be talking to another human person trying to survive in today's economy. Explain what you want to accomplish, that you need to restructure your debt and arrive at an agreement based on your new economic situation. You are closing the account and have a limited income for paying off creditors. Explain how you have arrived at the figure you are offering to pay. In the example above, you would offer $127.50 a month for 60 months to Capitalism Two to pay off the debt. If the representative can accept the arrangement, get the new terms in writing. Over the course of five years you will pay back $7650 if the company agrees to accept the sum and stop charging compound interest on the account you are closing. This is the goal you need to keep in mind as you negotiate. You want financial freedom in five years.

The first time you contact creditors it is quite likely they will reject your offer to restructure your debts. From their perspective, you have a track record of being a valued customer. For many months you have been handing over money and they will initially assume this relationship ought to continue for decades into the future, maybe the rest of your working life. Initially the corporate representative is likely to reject your offer and refuse to negotiate. At this point, they simply may not believe that you are serious.

How should you respond when they reject your offer? Now is when you must really decide if you are leaving Babylon behind. If you are, close the account and find out the exact amount owed at this point in time. Record this information because you will need it later. Follow up the conversation with a letter summarizing your offer, the amount you owe, and the fact that you closed the account with an outstanding balance of a particular sum. Explain that you regret their decision to reject your offer and are willing to reopen negotiations at a later date. Be certain to send a copy of this letter to the correct address for correspondence with the company. Be sure you do not send it to the address for payments. In order to leave Babylon, you must now stop making minimum payments to this creditor. Instead, deposit the sum you were negotiating to give them in an earmarked savings account. If Capitalism Two will not negotiate debt restructuring at this point in time, do not send them any money at all. If you continue making minimum payments you are accepting the terms of the prior arrangement. If you send them less they want under, they will take the money, and charge late fees and raise your interest rates too. What happens next is discussed in the next chapter.

In turn, call every creditor and ask for debt restructuring

based on what you can afford to pay. Creditors who accept the offer you make should be paid every month as agreed and on time. If, and only if, your gross income declines substantially should you revisit arrangements made with the companies that accepted the offer to pay them off in five years.

Strategy for Funding your Escape

What happens with the money earmarked for paying off debts to companies not willing to accept it? As you make regular deposits into a special savings account, preferably at a credit union across town, the funds will accumulate over time. Be patient and let the sum of money in the account increase. Do not make partial payments as this will not help you. The company will take your money, raise interest rates and charge late fees. It is not to your advantage to throw good money after bad. No doubt the creditor will contact you by phone and sending letters. Each time they call, repeat the offer and explain to each new corporate representative who calls. If you did your homework, you volunteered to give them all they would get should they go to court to obtain a judgment and garnish your wages. You are volunteering to save them the effort. After you understand the state law that governs these matters, you know what they can take from your wages. They can choose to take their share or not. You have no control over what they decide to do. What you cannot do is allow yourself to be bullied into giving them more than what is lawful. The state you live in determined how much of an individual's wages can be garnished to satisfy various judgments. You are simply offering to live up to the letter of the law. Are corporations entitled to continue to collect compound interest if they get a judgment? Most likely they would only get simple interest on a judgment and you could, over time, pay this off.

If a company continues to reject your offer and refuses to negotiate, it will eventually declare your (closed) account to be in default and will turn it over to collections. Normally when customers don't make payments on revolving debts the company closes the account and turns it over to collections, but you already closed the accounts. Collection is a process and each company has its own method. Often the debt first goes to an in-house collections department. Stand your ground when discussing the debt with the collections department. Nothing has changed. You made a good faith offer to restructure debt and they rejected it. Shift the burden back to them to make a counter offer but remember the principles on which your offer is based. The collections department may refer you to a credit counseling service. It could be useful for you to discuss your income and outgo with this specialist and go over your budget. If you have adopted a budget as proposed earlier, there is not much room for you to make higher payments than you have offered. Referring you to talk to a specialist can be a means for the collections department to discover how much you make and how you spend your money. Based on the conversation with the credit counseling specialist, the collections department might decide to take your offer. If they do, get the agreement in writing. You want the debt to be settled and ideally you want it to say 'paid' on your credit report too.

Time is your friend. You can have the same conversation with a collection agent every month. The collections agent has to comply with rules about when they can call your home and they cannot call you at work without your permission. They cannot harass you, but they can be persistent. Be firm, there isn't anything you can do to improve your offer unless you get a raise. As long as your financial situation remains consistent, the lawful percentage of your wages that could be garnished is what you can afford to divide among your creditors.

If the house collection department gives up trying to get money from you, the debt may be sold to another company, a collection agency. The company from whom you originally borrowed money reduces its tax liability by writing off the debt. Once the debt is purchased by a third party collection agency, you have new opportunities to negotiate. This is why you want to continue to set aside a monthly sum for liquidating the debt. Now you might be able to settle the debt for 10 to 25 cents on the dollar amount of the original debt. The original debt is the sum you owed the day you closed the account and ceased to be a customer of the original lender, not the amount they created after you closed the account. Be insistent on this figure. On the $12,000 debt to Capitalism Two that has been sold to this new company, being by offering to pay 10 percent or $1200 cash to settle the account. If you have been making regular payments into an earmarked account it is quite likely you will have this much available by the time you are talking to a third party collection agency. Do not offer to pay any more money to settle this account than what you have saved already for this purpose. If the third party collection agency rejects the 10 percent offer, next month you will have accumulated a little more and you can offer that amount. Eventually the amount of money you offer will finally be acceptable to the collection agency. Each passing month increases the sum you have saved which is available for negotiating with collection agencies. Time is on your side. Open your negotiations by offering the amount earmarked for this particular debt. By the time the account has been turned over to a collection agency, it is likely that 12 or more months will have passed which is why 10 percent is an appropriate opening offer. If the collection agency refuses to settle for this amount, they will contact you next month. At that time, you can offer a little more.

It never makes sense dip into emergency savings until

you have a reserve equal to more than six months of your gross income, or ideally a year. This is how much money you ought to have saved for emergencies in the event you are injured, laid off, or unable to work for some reason. You need another reserve fund for predicable events such as the furnace breaking down or the roof springing a leak or a filling falling out. Scriptures commands us to make it our ambition to work to have to give to those in need, so it makes sense to also have an account set aside for the purpose of sharing with the less fortunate when they are in need. Until you have set aside funds for these purposes, you cannot afford to dip into savings to pay off old debts. Pay off old debts from the funds you set aside exclusively for that purpose.

Be sure that each creditor and collection agency realizes you are in negotiations with all creditors and will prioritize those with whom you reach an agreement to restructure debt and settle accounts. Keep a dedicated journal near the phone so you can make notes on each conversation you have with creditors. This might be an important paper trail in the event you need documentation. Get the name of the individual with whom you discuss the account, note the date and time of day of the conversation. The company is probably recording the conversation and you might want to be able to access it too. Get the individual's company identification number, their department, and so forth as these are the details can enable you to subpoena records. Jot down notes of what is discussed. Always be truthful, let your yes be yes and your no be no, but remember you do not need to divulge intimate details about your personal life to complete strangers over the phone. As appropriate, send follow up letters referencing the conversation. Keep a file with all correspondence sent and received by date as you may eventually need to demonstrate that you made a good faith effort to arrive at an agreement. Send important documents certified mail so a human being has to sign for them. Double check addresses where you send communication and payments. Consider a voice recording of any conversations and offer a disclaimer that you are recording the conversation for quality assurance (just like they do). Keep an impeccable record of your efforts to be responsible while digging yourself out of debt. Yes, this requires some diligence, but it is a priceless education.

If a creditor takes you to court in order to reduce an outstanding debt to a judgment, do not let this frighten you. The primary reason a creditor would do this is because otherwise a statute of limitations would make it impossible for them to collect on the debt. If the amount in controversy is more than $20 you have the right to ask for a jury. The jury may be interested in the fact that you made a good faith effort to settle the debt outside of the judicial setting. Courtrooms are for obtaining justice and you do not need to be afraid. The court will likely conclude that you owe money, but you already know you owe money.

You need to understand how the credit laws work. If Capitalism Two refuses to negotiate a deal and you stop making payments to them, it should be because they refused their fair share of what the law says you can afford to pay. When they declare the debt to be in default, it becomes a black mark on your credit history for a period of seven years. If you start making monthly payments on this defaulted debt the clock is extended each time you make a payment. In light of this rather ludicrous truth, your credit report will be better off if you stop paying at all than pay a little every month on a defaulted account.

If you are dealing with a collection agency, you want to negotiate a lump sum payment to settle the account. Never borrow money to pay off a debt. Never consider missing a mortgage payment to pay off a consumer debt. Do not agree to make payments to the collection agency as this prolongs the black mark on your credit report. Your first concern is to pay off debts to individuals and corporations that accepted your debt restructuring plan. Let the others go to the back of the line. If you owe individuals money, you need to have this in writing to protect them so they can have a place in line if necessary in garnishment proceedings.

Will taking this approach hurt your credit score? Certainly it will. Should your behavior be determined by fear of a bad credit score? How much of your life are you willing to spend cowering before the beast? Corporations can unilaterally hurt your credit score without you doing anything. By dropping the limit on your lines of credit the bankers can negatively impact your debt to credit ratio. This ratio constitutes more than a third of the data on which your credit score is based. Since the bankers can manipulate your score on a whim, why do you care what your credit score is? *You care because you are being bombarded with a campaign designed to manipulate you into caring.* The credit score belongs to the beast. It is a score assigned by corporations to treat peoples as commodities. The score is controlled by corporations who collect data on human beings. The fancy mathematical formulas for scoring are made up by statisticians who work for the corporations.

It is time someone states the obvious, the mathematical voodoo used to generate credit scores is not open to scrutiny by reputable mathematicians, and it is not subject to peer review. Peer review is a critically important element in the progress of science. Scientists publish their work in peer reviewed journals; they explain their methods and their results to peers who can challenge the veracity of the information. Other scientists review both the methods and the mathematical analyses provided in scientific articles. Scientists decide whether or not information is credible. The formulas for generating credit scores are proprietary, which means they are not subject to scrutiny by disinterested parties. The validity of the numbers cannot be challenged. What we have is a number assigned to us that no one gets to cross check. There is nothing scientific about this process; it is an illusion designed simply to generate revenue for corporations, beginning with selling information and credit scores. If and when Middle America realizes the nature of this scam and revolts against it in substantial numbers, the tyranny will end.

Remember, you care about your credit score because you are being bombarded with a campaign to make you care. The score is being used to manipulate human behavior. If you are neglecting your spiritual life in order to make payments you cannot afford, you are being manipulated. If you are not donating money to provide for the poor because you feel you must make meet minimum payments to corporations instead, you are being manipulated. Some behaviors are governed by nature and nature's God. Natural law dictates that we care for our dependents and have compassion on the suffering of the less fortunate. Laws of commerce that allow money to be lent at usury interest are not naturel law; these laws exist because mercantile powers created them. Money is not natural. What happens if you get a bad credit score? You either cannot borrow money at all or you must pay exorbitant interest rates to borrow. If you have repented of living in Babylon, this does not matter. It does not matter because you no longer worship Mammon and the god of this world.

If there is one truth you need to take away from reading this book, it is this: Your credit score matters only if you intend to continue doing business with the beast. If you have repented and want to pack up and head out of Babylon, your credit score is irrelevant. If a substantial number of honest, hardworking, middle class Americans decide they will not be tyrannized by credit scores, the scores will become meaningless for distinguishing between us and this will help the poor among us.

Assume two individuals have the same poor credit score of 580. One of these individuals is a con artist who seldom earns a paycheck. He moves frequently and skips out on bills. The other individual works at a low paying job and lives within her means. Her bad score is the result of losing a better paying job which caused her to miss payments as she is having substantial difficulty making ends meet. There is a relevant moral distinction in character between these two individuals, but the score doesn't reflect it. Now consider the upper middle class American who reads this book and decides he is tired of the tyranny of the establishment. He had a credit score of 720 before he decided it was wrong to ignore the mission appeal at church to help the poor in Haiti after the earthquake. He has decided to stop financing an affluent lifestyle and to live a much more modest existence. He no longer regards his credit score as the most important number in his life. Now he shares the 580 credit score with the other two individuals. These three souls all have the same mark, and the beast cannot distinguish between them. God can.

Next time you are on the phone with a bill collector, you might ask them why you need to comply with what they want. Listen carefully as they will bring up your credit score and the notion of improving or protecting it. Tell them you don't care about your credit score and then really listen to what they say as they attempt to persuade you that you should care deeply about your credit score.

As you go through the process of negotiating your freedom from the beast, agents for banks and corporations are sitting in front of computer screens accessing information about your life. The agent sees files from credit reporting agencies on you. He has your home phone number and mailing address. Likely he knows where you work. He probably has access to information in your credit report that you have never seen. He knows how much you pay each month for utilities. He may know where you take your children to day care. Did you give this stranger permission to access this information?

Always be honest about your financial situation. You make a certain amount of money that is reported by your employer to the IRS. You have offered to pay your creditors the lawfully collectable portion of your disposable income to satisfy your debts as best you can in a reasonable time. All you can do is your best. Meanwhile, you should be living modestly and prudently to gain your economic freedom. The agent speaking with you on the phone has a fairly accurate idea of how you spend your monthly income.

The relationship you have with creditors who produce money unconstitutionally is governed by man's laws. You have no eternal, moral obligations to banks. The Sovereign King of highest heaven never endorsed the idea of profiting from lending money at usury interest rates. The laws that apply to these transactions are not divinely sanctioned; they were made here on earth. If the legal system says 10 percent of your disposable income can be garnished for debts, this is what you need to pay to be a law-abiding citizen. Granted the banks might like more, but heaven does not require you to give more.

Contentment

Borrowing money to buy consumer goods represents a lack of contentment with your circumstances. Repent of any sinful behavior that contributed to your current financial difficulties. Repentance means changing your mind and not engaging in the sinful behavior any more. Once you repent, you can live at peace. You do not need to be anxious, depressed and stressed over debts. You have a plan and are giving your creditors their fair share of your income each month. Sleep peacefully because you are doing what the law requires, you do not need to do more. If you try and give the creditors more than the amount state law requires, you are likely to keep borrowing money to meet expenses and this is a trap. Do not let yourself be caught in the trap of economic slavery. You must live on less than you make each month. You must set aside money for emergencies, ideally at least ten percent of your income. Do not pay creditors more than what the law requires until you have saved at least one year of income. Do not pay banks more than what the law demands if you do not honor God with the first fruits of your income by dividing your bread with the poor. Do the corporations who trashed the world's economy deserve more than God? Do they deserve more than what the law requires? These are soulless corporations. They are not deities. Do not bow down in homage to multinational corporations. Stop living in fear of them.

Men and women of good conscience have a difficult time grasping this, but the multinational corporation that extended credit is not like Aunt Matilda who took hard earned currency out of her cookie jar to lend to you. The banks fabricated the money they loaned consumers by issuing lines of credit; they inflated the currency and traumatized the world's economy in the process of striving to achieve their prime directive. Your Aunt Matilda doesn't have a printing press in the basement does she? Therein lays a relevant distinction between corporations issuing consumer credit cards and real people lending money to friends and relatives. Educate yourself about the difference between the money the constitution gives Congress the right to coin and the plastic that passes for money presently.

Above all else, you need to change the way you think about money. Leaving Babylon means you must stop living on credit. Pay yourself first. It does not make sense for you to borrow money at interest to pay off debts. You already owe money, why borrow more money? If you are in debt you have already borrowed more money than you ought to have borrowed. Negotiate a cash settlement only if it makes financial sense and only if the creditor puts the agreement in writing in advance of payments. Otherwise you run the risk the collection agency will take the money and still declare the balance outstanding. You want accounts reported as "paid" or "paid as agreed" in your credit report. Hold out for a written agreement with a human signature if possible.

Educate yourself about the Fair Credit Reporting Act. If an original creditor decides to treat a debt as uncollectible because it has been 180 days since your last payment, the creditor may "charge off" the account. This means the original creditor will treat the debt as uncollectible. This creates a black mark on your credit report for seven years. It will hurt your credit score, but that is far less important than saving an emergency fund.

When a creditor "charges off" an account, it means the creditor is writing the debt off to obtain a tax benefit. Once a creditor defaults a debt, do not make another payment on that debt to any entity until you can settle it completely. Outside collection agencies and law offices collect debts for a commission of 15-25% of the sum they manage to collect after the debt is charged off. Collection agencies do not have an infinite amount of time to collect the money from you. Rules about wage garnishment apply to collection agencies that buy debts. If an unscrupulous firm takes you to court when you are doing your best, invite all your other creditors to participate in the proceedings too. There is no point in letting the most unscrupulous firm have first place in line. If you demonstrate that you have been honest with your creditors and have been making payments to the best of your ability to the maximum amount allowed by state law, you might find a sympathetic judge and jury. The judge might decide the unscrupulous firm should not get any money at all in a wage garnishment proceeding. Learn your rights and represent yourself. Basically there is just one line in which all regular creditors must stand to get their share of a fixed percent of your income, perhaps ten percent of your gross. If creditors loaned you so much they are not happy with their share of this sum, they were probably being greedy. Or perhaps your economic circumstances have changed with the downturn in the ecology; in which case lenders were foolish in thinking they could predict the future. But whether they were greedy or foolish, it is not your problem.

As much as it lies within your power, you want to live a life of integrity and pay back what is lawfully required of you. If you have been making interest payments for years, you may be surprised to know you probably paid back what you borrowed several times over already. If you are in serious economic trouble, consider the option of option of bankruptcy. Pray about it and study want the bible says about the year of jubilee. Like garnishment laws, bankruptcy is part of civil law that governs what belongs to Caesar. There are situations in which people must avail themselves of bankruptcy laws if they are ever to be free of economic slavery. Why does bankruptcy carry such negative connotations in our society now? The bankruptcy laws in the United States are modeled after the laws of Israel when God was King. God is gracious and forgiving of debts. God has called us to peace.

If you cannot afford to pay back late fees, over limit fees, and ridiculously high interest rates arbitrarily imposed by the banks, don't. These are not sanctioned by heaven. Here is an example: Suppose you have a credit card with a $2,000 limit and charge $1,000 on it. One day the bank decides to drop your credit limit to $1,050 and to raise your interest rate from 9.99 percent to 24.44 percent. With the new interest rate, it may be that the card goes over its limit and the bank assess an over limit fee. Perhaps the bank even changed the due date on the card so your automatic payment arrived late. The bank gets to charge interest on the late fee too. Imagine that you have been faithfully making your monthly payments on time for years. Why allow yourself to be treated this way? Call the company and ask to have the fees removed. If the company refuses, cancel the account and never do business with the company again. It is not acceptable to treat people with callous disregard. Call the company two or three times a week if you need to and tell them you refuse to pay the fees. If a department store card treats you badly, cancel the card and stop shopping at the store. We need to stop behaving like junkies who will do absolutely anything for our next fix of credit. The image of the harlot is not far from the truth when people behave like credit whores willing to be treated any way for money.

The US Congress has passed new legislation to protect consumers from many of the most reprehensible practices of lenders. In the small interval of time before these new laws became binding on the banks, the banks implemented various strategies to insure their profits. For example, banks intend to charge customers who do not carry outstanding balances a yearly fee just for having a credit card. The banks believe customers will pay this new fee rather than close accounts and negatively impact credit scores. Should anyone allow banks to treat them this way? Isn't this a form of blackmail? Notice the banks presume we have no choice but to do business with them. If we have money saved for emergencies, banks cannot treat us like this.

Taking a case to court is expensive. As long as you are doing the best you can, do not be intimidated by threats about a court action. If a court sees that you have been voluntarily paying the lawful portion of your income towards your debts, what more can a judge order? The only debtors' prison we have in the United States is self-imposed. We mentally grovel at the feet of the beast in fear that it won't like us. Get over fear that the banks won't like you. You only need banks to like you if you intend to stay in Babylon. Getting out of Babylon is a command, not a suggestion. Do not be afraid of the threat that your credit score will be ruined if you close accounts. If you are not a customer you should not be paying interest and fees. If you are not a customer you can negotiate a debt settlement. Once you are not a customer, they bank is no longer performing a service for you.

A credit score takes credit utilization into account. To have a good score, you can only have 10-30 percent of your total credit limit outstanding as debt. The banks decide what your credit limit will be, so banks may manipulate your credit score. If they offer you a credit card with $1,000 limit and you only charge $100 on it that would contribute to a good credit score; but the bank can arbitrarily lower your credit limit to $105 and that will hurt your credit score. Banks can raise your interest rates for any reason they like or no reason at all. Department stores charge phenomenally high rates for their cards, like 24.99%. You do not need to be an economic slave to these companies.

Your goal is to be free. Your goal is to be a free human being and be treated as such rather than as a commodity for corporations. Stop bowing down in fear to the beastly system running the world economy. We are not going to be free of the beastly way corporations treat people until we grasp the fact we do not need them. Rather, they need us. Banks do not produce anything. The money that banks make comes from lending money at interest. What happens if we stop borrowing money from them? They won't have any money, will they? That might eventually reduce the power they hold over us.

Do we need to buy any more stuff on credit? Americans have plenty of material possession already. We can buy and sell it to each other in thrift stores, at garage sales, on EBay and Craig's List for the next 100 years. We can barter and we can trade. We do not need to buy more consumables produced by slave labor in foreign nations, consumables purchased with money loaned to us at ridiculous interest rates. It is time for us to get over the materialism that is rotting the fabric of our civilization. We need to be content whether we have a little or plenty.

We have to be able to differentiate between our needs, our wants and our desires. We need a bowl of rice to sustain physical life; we might want meatloaf or desire dinner out. Are you willing to give up your freedom and peace of mind for dinner at a five star restaurant? Are you willing to trade your birthright for a bowl of porridge?

By now you may wonder if you can buy a house if you leave Babylon. If you already own a house, you might want to stay put. Take care of it, pay it off, and give your children and grandchildren a home that is not mortgaged. If you do not already own a house and think it might be prudent to purchase one, how about finding an owner who will carry the loan on a contract for deed? Maybe your parents need to sell their house? Pay the owner of the home you are purchasing the interest you would have paid the bank on the mortgage. The owner can hold the deed for security. If you don't pay, he gets his house back, along with all the money you have paid. Do we really need to keep paying the banks interest on the same houses over and over again, which is exactly what we have been doing. We don't own our houses, we rent them from banks. We are serfs in our own homes. Let us stop this nonsense. If we put money in savings accounts the bankers pay us tiny sums of interest, but they loan money to us it is at double digit interest rates. How about helping a relative pay off their mortgage if you have money to invest? You will make more in interest than the banks will give you, won't you? We need to rethink the way we live economically. We need to trust people more than financial institutions.

What happened to families living together and helping each other out? This is the only nation on earth where multiple generations do not live together in a home the family owns. One of the few good things that may come from the present economic crisis is that it may bring back the extended family. Think about it, grown children can move in with their parents and help pay off the mortgage. The parents can take off to Florida and leave their adult children with a house with no mortgage. Of course this would require that we learn how to live with one another. Would that be such a bad idea?

Most of all do not be afraid that you will hurt your credit score by breaking free of economic serfdom. Accept the fact that the credit score is a beastly idea. If you cower in fear of having a bad credit score, your fear is misplaced. The bible is clear on this: *Fear Him who is able to cast both body and soul into hell.* Fear God, stop fearing corporations and the consequences of them marking you with a bad score.

To get out of Babylon, you must learn to be content on with what you earn. You must live within your means. Give ten percent of your income towards paying off your creditors and save ten percent against future needs. Once you have a little money saved, make loans to yourself at 12% interest if you must buy something not in your budget, perhaps tires for the car or a washing machine. Charge yourself late fees if you don't make your monthly payment on time. Treat yourself like the banks have been treating you and you will get rich. Most of all invest ten percent of your income in helping others; advance the Kingdom of God if you are one of its citizens. It you do not believe in the reign of heaven, give a portion of your wealth to care for the less fortunate anyway. This ten percent is what sanctifies the rest of your finances and gives life meaning.

Learn to live on seventy percent of your disposable income even if that means eating rice and making your own laundry soap. You might need to move into a smaller place or share the place you have with someone else to make ends meet. Happiness is never found in things. Happiness comes from experiences and enjoying relationships with people. A bowl of soup in peace is better than a feast washed down with anxiety over how to pay the supper bill. .

Your goal is freedom from financial tyranny. It is tyranny when international bankers can manipulate the US government into giving billions of dollars to banks, debt that your grandchildren will be repaying. It is tyranny when bankers manipulate credit scores so they can charge outrageous interest rates on old debts. The banks are not going to repossess the shoes charged on your credit card. The shoes were never collateral; the bankers don't want the shoes. The banks want you and the fruit of your labor; you are the collateral. They want you to be perpetually in debt to them. You are just a commodity to them, a commodity from which they can profit as they buy and sell your future. The bankers get you to participate in the present evil world system by the threat of a bad credit score. Your credit score won't matter once you come out of Babylon. Stop borrowing money to buy material things you don't need; stop selling your future; stop living beyond your means. Be content in your circumstances. Trust God.

Deceptions of the Beast

Once you have reached the decision to leave Babylon and achieve freedom from economic slavery you might like help. Legitimate non-profit consumer credit counseling services are a place to start. A legitimate one will require credit cards to be destroyed and accounts to be closed. Depending on individual circumstances, they may be able to negotiate lower interest rates on accounts. The service will handle paperwork, which can be very helpful. The creditor sends in a monthly payment to the consumer credit counseling service, and it dispenses payments to creditors. The service charges a modest monthly fee for its work on your behalf. A consumer credit counseling service can provide a measure of protection for folks who would otherwise be taken advantage of by collections departments. It can be a great relief to have knowledgably help while digging out of debt. Be aware there are companies which pass themselves off as serving consumers that are fronts for banks and collection agencies. Before working with one of these services, do your homework about them.

Debt settlement companies are another matter. These are businesses out to profit on people's misery. Several states have made these businesses illegal. A debt settlement company cannot do anything you could not do for yourself. These businesses have advertisements running on radio stations across the nation. If you contract for their services, they are likely to instruct you to stop paying creditors and send the money to them instead. They collect a hefty percent of your entire debt as a fee, and then they will make some sort of effort to negotiate settlements with your creditors using the rest of the money you've given them. Debt settlement companies do not promise to keep creditors from filing suits for judgments. Debt settlement can be a taxable event. Be aware that if you are in a 15 percent tax bracket, having $5,000 of debt forgiven could mean you owe an additional $750 in taxes. Being aware of this possibility makes it possible to be prepared.

When negotiating with a creditor or collection agency to settle a debt, pay with a cashier's check. Otherwise they will have your bank account information. On the face of the check write a note that indicates that if the check is cashed it settles the account in full. Keep a photocopy of the face of the check. As part of any settlement agreement, request the account be reported to credit reporting agencies as *paid in full* rather than *paid according to agreement*. Ask to have this agreement in writing and obtain it before you make the payoff. The creditor or collection agency needs to state in writing that you do not owe taxes on the forgiven debt. If you are insolvent, meaning your outstanding debt if greater than your worth, the Internal Revenue Service does not tax debt forgiveness. Presumably you are insolvent if you are negotiating debt restructuring and settlements; otherwise you could use assets to pay off accounts. Additionally, you want written assurance from a collection agency that the original creditor cannot come after the debt at any time in the future. Get these points in writing, and save the paperwork.

Perhaps the debt you owe is to the federal government. A federal agency can require an employer to deduct up to 15% of disposable pay for debts owed to the government. Disposable pay means compensation, including salary, bonuses, commissions, vacation pay, and so forth, after deductions such as health insurance premiums, federal, state, and local taxes. Federal law says that everyone is entitled to keep an amount equal to at least 30 times the federal minimum wage each week. If you can manage on less than $11,000 a year disposable income, you are below the garnishment line, because you are at the poverty line. In the event you owe the federal government and other creditors, the total garnishment cannot exceed 25 percent of your disposable or take home income, providing this doesn't put you under the $11,000 a year. Federal law 31 U.S.C. § 3720D(e) makes it illegal for an employer to fire an employee just because wages are garnished, at least the first time garnishment occurs. The law is ambiguous regarding subsequent garnishments.

The Federal Trade Commission (FTC), the nation's consumer protection agency, enforces the Fair Debt Collection Practices Act (FDCPA), which prohibits debt collectors from using abusive, unfair, or deceptive practices to collect. Debt collectors include collection agencies, lawyers who collect debts, and the companies that buy delinquent debts. The Act covers most personal and household debts, on everything from credit cards, to auto loans, to medical bills and mortgages. It does not cover debts incurred in the operation of a business.

Sometimes people find out that high medical bills have been run up in their name because someone stole their identity. Medical identity theft occurs when someone uses your identifying information to obtain medical treatment or medical supplies. The person may have been desperate when they stole your name or insurance card, but you can find yourself harassed with the medical debt, erroneous negative data on your credit report, and far worse, false information on medical records that could be life threatening. Medical identity theft can also involve false claims filed to a victim's health insurance plan. Medical identity theft represents just one more way we become victims by having our information stored in computer data files.

Unless you are extremely good at negotiating, you may not want to negotiate terms over the telephone as you talk to collection agents. Remember they are professionals and spend their days collecting debts. They are trained to collect money and are fairly good at it if they still work in collections. Collection agencies have preferences about what they want:

> Balance in full,
> Settlement (in no more than two payments),
> Payments over 3 or more months, usually not to exceed 6 months,
> Good faith payment while you ask others for loan.

The goal of all the efforts by the collection agencies representative is to get as much money as possible as quickly as they can. They will tend to refuse your offers and may try to manipulate you into accepting their terms. Make your offer once or twice. If it is refused, end the conversation. Remember you cannot go further into debt, so never consider borrowing money to pay off a consumer debt. Having studied the state laws that pertain to judgment and wage garnishments, you are empowered with facts. You understand how much money state law exempts from garnishment each month and how much is available for liquidating debts. This is the basis for your negotiations. There is no point and no justice in accepting a worse deal for yourself than a court would give you.

Be absolutely certain the Statute of Limitations does not apply to the debt before agreeing to pay anything. Often any payment or a written agreement to pay could serve to restart the statute of limitations clock on a debt. If you want to settle a debt that is in default, it is best to set aside money until you are capable of making a single lump sum payment to clear up the debt entirely. Keep the money you are earmarking to settle the debt in your possession as it accumulates. The only exception to make to this general rule is in the event a collection agency agrees in writing to settle a debt for a very small percent of the total owed on the condition you make two payments. The collection agency would most likely have accepted the same sum of money in one payment as half the amount in two payments. By keeping the money in your possession until you can clear the debt entirely, you are protecting yourself.

The representative for the collection agency has a preference for how he would like to receive your payment. He prefers:

1. To be able to withdraw money from your bank account via post-dated checks or automatic electronic withdrawals.
2. Priority Mail
3. Certified Mail

There is no legal requirement to allow collection agents to have access to your bank account, through posted dated checks or otherwise. It is never a good idea to postdate checks because they can be cashed and your bank account can be overdrawn in the process. Do not be intimidated into letting them into your account. Pay by a method that does not provide information about your bank account, use a postal money order or bank draft sent by official mail. Before sending the collection agency any money, be certain you have a signed agreement from it in your possession that can stand up in a court of law. Keep accurate records of agreements, and this could include a tape recording of the conversation.

Just like the collectors have priorities when they conduct business, you have priorities to keep clearly in mind while you resolve your financial affairs. Approach matters rationally rather than emotionally. It may not be in your best interest to negotiate any payment agreements if you have limited funds and need the money to provide for biological necessities, like food, heat in the winter, or a place to sleep. It is also not in your best interest to pay a debt if the statute of limitations has expired or is about to expire. Remember, a single payment can reset the statute of limitations and give the creditor six additional years to file a lawsuit. The statute of limitations is the period of time that a creditor or collector can use the court to collect a debt. The time period starts on the account's last date of activity and varies by state. It is important for you to identify the date of the last payment you make on an account as well as when the account is closed. The date of the last activity on an account can be different from when the account went past due or in default. Statute of limitations is generally between 3 and 6 years, but as high as 15 years in some states. The statute of limitations on debts is different than the time a delinquent debt can be reported on a credit report, which is typically 7 years from the date of a delinquency. Bankruptcies are reported for 10 years and tax liens for 15. Federal student loans, child support and some state income taxes have not statute of limitations. If you move from one state to another, the statute which applies is the one from the state where you were living when the account had its last activity. Never pay if the debt is the result of identity theft. Do not pay debts if you subsist on money that is exempt from collection because it comes from a protected source such as Social Security, Public Assistance, the Veterans Administration, child support, or a pension. Emotionally you may feel that you should be paying, but rationally your first priority is to achieve financial stability in the present, after which you can address the past.

Be realistic about your budget. Disposable income is all that you have to work with to liquidate debts. If you are giving ten percent and saving ten percent, you can afford to give ten percent towards old debts. Should you prioritize paying off old debts over helping others survive in the present? Priorities after these expenses are food and a place to shelter that is within your means. When negotiating, determine how much money is available for debt liquidation and offer less than this amount. This will provide you with room for negotiating. Never agree to pay more than you can afford. That is the road that lead to the financial difficulties you now face.

Debt collectors are most likely to settle for a partial payment in a lump sum. The best time to negotiate debt settlement is at the end of the month. Collection agents are paid commissions based on their collections during the month. There is probably no need for you to tell your story to the collection agent, they do not offer deals out of sympathy. Understand garnishment laws and knowing the collection agent has access to your credit report may help you frame your offer. Being factual can prove helpful.

In the event you cannot make payments or offer funds to settle debts you need to watch for court papers to arrive in the mail. Never ignore legal papers as you must respond to the court. If any creditor or collection agency goes to court without serving notice to you, they will obtain a default judgment against you because you did not appear. You can get this judgment vacated and set aside for failure to serve you. You cannot get it set aside if you ignored the legal paperwork. Do not let the idea of going to court frighten you. The creditor or collection agency is merely reducing what is owed to a legal judgment for the sake of collecting rather than letting the statute of limitations run. It may well be to your advantage if the debt is reduced to a judgment amount at a simple interest rate rather than continue on accumulating double digit compound interest. A $5000 debt at 24 percent compound interest can never be paid off by a debtor who is only making the minimum payment on the account. Paying off a $5000 judgment with a simple interest rate of 9 percent can be accomplished in just five years by making monthly payments of $104. Creditors may decide to go to court as judgment extends the length of time they have to collect by up to 20 years. The good news is that this is rather irrelevant as the total amount they can collect each month is fixed by state law.

Even if a consumer debt has expired because the six years elapsed and it was never reduced to a judgment, collection agencies can still contact you and try and get you to pay the debt. A collection agency could even go to court and sue you for the old debt that is past the statute of limitations. If you appear in court in this case, merely showing the statute of limitations has run on the debt will get the case dismissed in your favor. If you fail to appear in court, you could lose and end up liable for the debt. Unless you went to court to get the erroneous judgment cancelled or vacated, the creditor could have twenty years to collect on the judgment it should never have been awarded. Courts are for obtaining justice. If you do not owe a debt, the court can help you. If you do owe a debt, the court is simply going to affirm this fact and may still help you by halting the compound interest that is enslaving. Civil courts are for settling difficulties between parties. We are perhaps afraid of courts because we do not have teams of lawyers and lots of experience with courts.

Questioning the Mark

We have facilitated our own destruction by allowing corporations to use social security numbers for record keeping purposes. These numbers enable corporations to maintain and share records on us. Facilitating corporate invasion of private lives of real people was not the original intent of the numbers. The Social Security Act of 1935 can be reviewed on-line at a web site maintained by the federal government - www.socialsecurity.gov. The original act did not include any mention of the numbers which are now so widely used. It was the Treasury Department that issued numbers to workers covered by social security insurance to track their earnings and old age benefits. Back in those days our elected representatives might have intended to set the money aside, but the fund has been raided for decades.

The first version of social security cards stated plainly across their face that they were not to be used for identification purposes. That has certainly changed. The government itself decided the numbers could be used to identify taxpayers and the federal government gave state governments the right to use the numbers on applications for driver's licenses to facilitate collecting delinquent child support payments. The government cannot require a citizen to disclose a social security number without a specific legal basis for the request. Corporations get citizens to disclose their social security numbers by simply refusing to provide services or do business with people who refuse to provide it.

The social security number facilitates the use of computers for managing data records about people. The expanded uses for the number have been fueled by advances in technology. Computers are much better at numbers than names. Banks, credit bureaus, hospitals, fuel oil dealer and colleges now use social security numbers for identification, but a number of colleges are moving away from their use to identify students. Initially there was a system underlying the assignment of the numbers which changes beginning June 25, 2011. After that date social security numbers will be assigned randomly making it much more difficult for hackers to correctly guess someone's number. Most readers were born when the systematic method was in place and that represents a security risk.

The expansion of the use of social security numbers began decades ago with an executive order in 1943 which required Federal agencies to use it with a new record system. In 1961, the Civil Service commission began using it to identify federal employees. In 1962 the Internal Revenue Service started using it for identifying taxpayers. This led to its use by banks so they could disclose interest payments to the IRS. The number now serves as a national identification number since parents were forced to obtain social security numbers for any children they wished to declare as dependents for tax returns beginning in 1987.

In 1976 the number began to be used on driver's license applications and for motor vehicle registration purposes. In 1996 the "deadbeat dad law" required the number from anyone seeking a marriage or occupational license, or from anyone who was party to divorce decree or child support order. Basically this enabled the government to track men and women who might be inclined to skip out of paying child support. The government was seeking to recover a portion of the money paid out through the Aid to Families with Dependent Children program, more commonly called welfare. We have come to the sad state of affairs where federal agencies do not accept state issued driver's licenses as proof of identity unless it includes a social security number. This says a great deal about the status of states relative to the federal government. Rather than put your social security number on your driver's license, get a United States passport to prove citizenship. Only certain documents can be used as proof of citizenship, these include a certified birth certificate, consular birth report, a passport, or a Certificate of Naturalization or Certificate of Citizenship.

The following is taken from the Social Security online web site, *"A Social Security number is important because you need it to get a job, collect Social Security benefits and receive some other government services. Many other businesses, such as banks and credit companies, also ask for your number."* Just because a business asks for your social security number, does not mean you should give it to them without a little thought on the matter. Banks file earned interest reports with the IRS, which is why they ask for a social security number when you open an account. Here is a quote addressed to noncitizens on the social security website: *Lawfully admitted noncitizens can get many benefits and services without a Social Security number. You do not need a number to get a driver's license, register for school, obtain private health insurance, or to apply for school lunch programs or subsidized housing. Some organizations use Social Security numbers to identify you in their records. Most, however, will identify you by some other means if you request it. We cannot assign you a Social Security number solely so you can get a driver's license or a service that requires a credit check. Although many companies, such as banks and credit companies, may ask for your Social Security number, you are generally not required to provide one if you don't have one.* Noncitizens can also apply for an *Individual Taxpayer Identification Number* from the Internal Revenue Service. What if citizens asked for the same consideration from companies?

You should be very concerned about the security of your social security number. Researchers at Carnegie Mellon demonstrated that it is relatively easy to crack the number if you can find out when and where a person was born, information you may be sharing on Facebook. It might have been this demonstration that influenced the government to start assigning social security numbers randomly.

Did any of the legislation discussed give corporations the right to use your social security number? Yes and no. The local bank where you cash your paycheck has the right to ask for your social security number to go with your bank account, but it might accept an *Individual Taxpayer Identification Number* instead. It could be very inconvenient to live without a bank account as this would make it difficult to cash paychecks. Beyond the need to have a number to open a bank account, we have voluntarily given companies the right to use social security numbers for identification and thus allowed our lives to be digitally tracked at every turn. Maybe it's time ***we the people*** revoked the use of our social security numbers for any but the original purpose. At the present time the government treats social security as if it were another form of welfare and not like an insurance policy, so maybe there is no purpose? As of May, 2011 the government wants to stop issuing social security benefits checks, to save postage the government will either deposit checks electronically or provide recipients with a debit card that can be used to withdraw cash from selected ATMs.

What if we all stopped giving out our social security? What if we did not just write it on every application without thinking about the matter? What if ***We the People*** started enforcing the laws of our nation for ourselves? What if we just refused to play along? What if we stopped buying consumer goods on credit? What if we bailed ourselves out now that our duly elected Congressmen and Senators have bailed out the bankers and Wall Street? While we are at it, what if we all stopped doing business with companies that do not treat us fairly? What if we stopped being consumers of products and services we do not really need? What if we all went on strike against materialism? What if we refused to deal with beastly corporations that treat us as mere chattel? What if corporations could no longer use credit scores to distinguish between us and mistreat the poor?

God has promised that if we seek His Kingdom first, He will see to it that we have our needs fulfilled. He knows we need food and clothing. When we place our confidence in God who reigns in heaven, earthly banks matter very little. Confidence in God needs to extend to our health as well as to our finances. Americans currently pay ridiculous amounts of money for health care, 1 in 5 dollars in the US economy. Can the families you know afford to pay $1,200 a month just in case someone gets sick? Could that money be put to better use? It has been projected that that the cost of health care will soon rise to use 1 out of 2 dollars. That will happen about the same time 50 percent of adults have diabetes. Every form of media bombards us with advertisements for various drugs so we can ask doctors to prescribe them.

What is the worst thing that could happen if you did not have medical insurance? You could die, right? Guess what, we all die with or without health insurance, and afterwards we face judgment. We need to stop being afraid of heaven. Place more confidence in the Great Physician and less in health insurance and pharmaceutical companies. Modern medicine will not make us immortal. By any objective measure a godly lifestyle goes farther towards insuring health than money paid out in premiums. The health care crisis reflects the cost of the seven deadly sins. Much of what we pay for health care reflects a sin tax. If you cannot afford premiums for health insurance you run the risk of not being able to afford expensive medical treatment of course, but this is only a risk. You might never need expensive treatment. You could also pay premiums for decades and learn that the insurance company denies you benefits when you file claims. Health insurance companies, like all other corporations, exist to maximize profits for shareholders. Paying out money on claims is a cost of doing business, not the goal of the corporation. For this reason, these corporations have many strategies in place to avoid paying claims. Paying over a thousand dollars a month over an entire lifetime is quite a bit to subsidize the cost of gluttony, vice and intemperance. Insurance should be insurance against an unforeseen catastrophe. Getting old is not an unforeseen catastrophe, it happens to all of us unless we tragically die young. Having a yearly physical is not unforeseen event so why should we expect insurance to pay for routine care?

Psychological services must be covered now like medical and surgical services. The problem with psychological services is the lack of any objective standard for diagnosing many psychological problems. There will be no end of therapists prescribing themselves in the days ahead. Read books like *Selling Sickness* and grasp the magnitude of the problem we face. Food corporations fattening us up for slaughter by feeding us high fructose corn syrup, Transfatty acids, MSG, and growth hormones pumped into cattle. We consume a host of things we do not need that are not good for us. When we grow morbidly obese on the typical American diet, pharmaceutical corporations offer to help us out by providing expensive drugs to treat our ailments. If we decide to try and get out of this loop by adopting a healthier life style, other corporations stand ready to sell us bottled water out of a tap to drink.

Facing the Beast

Collecting debts is a business, sometimes large corporations have their own in-house collections department and sometimes debts are sold to another company. The collection agency may be getting a percentage of whatever they collect and sometimes they bought the debt. What would motivate a company to sell your debt? Most likely the debt was sold for some tax advantage. A person might be quite willing to pay off their debts and might even be able to do so at some reasonable, simple interest rate. The creditor may reject this notion outright and prefer to take the tax advantage rather than the money over time. It is all about maximizing profits. If you find yourself conversing with a representative from collections, determine who they represent exactly. They might be an employee of the company with whom you incurred the debt, in which case the Fair Debt Collection Practices do not apply. This is a set regulations and rules that govern third party collections, after the debt has been turned over to a collection agency or sold. Like any other complex game, in order to play you need to understand the rules.

Third party collection agencies are entities that were not a party to the original agreement between a borrower and lender. Third party agencies make 10 to 15 percent of whatever amount they manage to collect on an old debt. This provides the incentive for them to collect as much as possible. If a $5000 dollar debt gets defaulted and turned over to a third party collection agency, it might settle for $2500. The collection agency itself will make $250 to $325. Collection agencies use multiple strategies to get money, including sending out scary letters every ten days that tell you to pay the amount owed or risk collection action and if course these letter carry the threat of a negative credit report. If you did not pay the debt to the original lender, the account is already in default and has impacted your credit score. Is the collection agency really going to start court proceedings to collect $250? In some cases collection agencies are fronts for lawyers and they might start a proceeding to obtain a judgment, but it is unlikely this will be their first effort at collecting.

The original creditor wrote the defaulted debt off its taxes before turning the account over to third party collections. At a corporate tax rate of 34 percent, you can estimate the benefit to them. If the lender has been charging 15 percent interest on a $5000 loan, a borrower paying $100 a month will have repaid almost the sum borrowed by the end of the fourth year of making payments. But because of compound interest rates, will still owe the lender $3000 or so. The bank collects $4800 on loan payments over four years and then writes off this $3000, saving $1000 in taxes. The bank made $800 on the bad loan. Contrast this with a customer who deposits $5000 in an account with the bank which ears 1.5 percent interest. In four years, the customer will earn about $300 over the four years. These figures are approximate and do not reflect any penalties, yearly fees, or interest rate increases the bank might charge. If the third party collection agency manages to settle the defaulted debt, that original lender will declare its share as income and pay taxes on that sum. If the borrower settles the debt for $2000, the bank will make another $1100 in profit. Overall in just four years the bank will make more than $1900 profit on a loan of $5000 that went bad. This example is given to encourage readers to try and understand lending and borrowing as a business. This is a helpful perspective when talking to collection agents. It could be worthwhile to have a complete picture back through time of how much you have borrowed and how much you have paid in interest and principle. You might want to also consider fees and late charges. This is good information to have in mind when you offer to settle a debt. Be clear when conversing with the third party collection agency that you asked to have the debt restructured so you could pay it off and the offer was declined. The sum of money you should use is the amount owed when you closed the account. Ignore hypothetical interest after that date as you certainly do not owe any interest to this third party collection agency. If you are settling a debt with a third party collection agency, offer 10 to 25 cents on the dollar of the debt owed when you closed the account. If you have been saving money for paying off your debts, it is only a matter of time before you have the funds to make this offer. Meanwhile, do not throw good money after bad as giving small payments to collection agents just encourages them to harass you.

You may find it somewhat therapeutic to chat with to debt collectors. This can give you an opportunity to discuss the national economy and politics. There is no point in being angry with the collection agent who is just some poor soul working at a job he probably does not enjoy. Do not make promises and do not give out information about your private life or bank accounts to strangers. When it comes time to settle the debt you can express mail a cashier's check. If a collection agency starts court proceedings to reduce a debt to a judgment, it is most likely because they feel they are running out of time to collect the debt. One of the great blessings of living honestly financially is that you have nothing to fear. The court is not going to make you do more than you have already offered to do if you follow the plan suggested in this book. If you investigate the state laws where you reside, you will know how much of your disposable income ought to go to repaying debts. You will have arranged your finances understanding these laws as you prepare to exit Babylon.

If a collection agency does take you to court, invite your creditors as there is no good reason to let the greediest cut to the front of the line in a wage garnishment action. Have your records with you and show that you have been working a plan to repay your creditors. If you cannot afford attorney fees, you are not obligated to hire a lawyer. The burden of responsibility to see that you are treated fairly falls on the court. Do be sure you understand the law in your own state. Some states allow up to 25 percent of wages to be garnished to satisfy judgments while others do not allow any wages to be garnished except for child support, guaranteed student loans, and court ordered fines. These states include North Carolina, South Carolina, Pennsylvania, and Texas.

A court proceeding might mean a creditor gets a judgment and this could entitle it to go after assets such as the equity in automobiles or real estate or money in a bank account. An individual who is earnest about leaving Babylon who has assets that can be liquidated to satisfy debts should have done so before a court is involved. If selling an object can set you free, why wouldn't you? Life does not consist of possessions even when you have an abundance of possessions.

There is no debtor's prison in the United States. If creditors take you to court and garnish your wages, the court is still going to let you keep 75 to 90 percent of your disposable paycheck. Even with a judgment, there is a statute of limitations for debt collection. In many cases creditors would be far better off to have revolving consumer debts reduced to judgments at simple interest because they could eventually pay off the debts, with compound interest that might never be possible. At this point if you are in debt, you should be downsizing and simplifying your lifestyle. You cannot escape from Babylon if you try and take it with you.

Companies in the business of collections use behavioral science to extract money from commodities called consumers. One categorized creditors by type and trains collection agents in which strategy to use based on a profile which has been determined by a mathematical model applied to data about the debtor:

- the naïve debtor who just doesn't understand finances.
- the ignorant debtor who might like to overcome debt but isn't succeeding.
- the debtor who wants to overcome his debts but has no one to assist him
- the debtor who wants to pay his debt, but whose situation has changed
- the debtor who wants to pay his debt, but doesn't understand the process and whose financial situation has changed from past to present.
- the debtor who simply does not want to pay.

The representative is trained to interact with the debtor using a strategy that is deemed most likely to yield results depending on the profile. If the first tactic doesn't work, the agent will move on to the next most likely strategy.

There is a difference between having a desire to pay off debt and the ability to do so and this is an important distinction. Making minimum payments for decades on consumer debts with compound interest rates is economic slavery; it is not paying off debts. Never try and borrow your way out of debt and this includes borrowing from your own future. The only money that can be given to creditors is what is available today and it cannot include the money in reserve for emergencies. Living outside Babylon without borrowing necessitates savings.

What you have for old consumer debt is about ten percent of your income, no matter how much you wish there was more. When you talk with collection agency representatives, they need to be told you want to pay off your debts but lack the resources to do so. You can honestly tell them you hope financial circumstances will improve enabling you to settle your debts.

While this may all seem very bleak to you, remember the only debtors prisons in the United Sates are in our minds. Poverty is not a sin and neither is being in debt. Lack of contentment, greed, and covetousness are sins and may have contributed to debt. People who are not in debt may be equally guilty of these sins. Repent of the sin and deal with the consequences. There are many reasons people fall into debt and some have nothing to do with their own sin. It is a perversion of the gospel to assume the rich are righteous and the poor are unrighteous. A balance sheet is not a status report on the condition of the soul. Having a good credit score is not a measure of spiritual worthiness. Having an excellent credit score might simply mean a person is shrewd *as the sons of this age are more shrewd in relation to their own kind that the sons of light.*

Repentance is a change of mind followed by corresponding action. Be content with your circumstances and stop longing for Babylonian luxury goods. Bringing forth fruit consistent with repentance means behavior must conform to beliefs. Living contentedly within one's means may require a lifetime of frugality. Stay away from the trap of lusting after things that are a delight to the eyes

Financial relationships with creditors are covered by contract law which is Caesar's domain. Contract law is not an extension of natural law neither is it divinely sanctioned. When God was king over ancient Israel, He did not permit lending money at usury interest to those in need. Commercial enterprises are covered in this passage, *Come now, you who say,*

'Today or tomorrow we will go to such and such a city, and spend a year there and engage in business and make a profit.' Yet you do not know what your life will be like tomorrow. You are just a vapor that appears for a little while and then vanishes away. (James 4:13-14). None of us can predict or control the future and for this reason it is not prudent to borrow against it. The verse which follows immediately after this one says, *"there is only one Lawgiver and Judge, the One who is able to save and to destroy; but who are you who judge your neighbor?"* What is a credit score but a judgment? The proverb, *'the borrower becomes servant to the lender'* is a warning about a danger; it does not represent divine sanction for enslaving the poor.

An individual who repents and determines to live within their means does not need to live in a psychological prison. It is better to be content with little than to have great wealth with unhappiness. Wealth is not synonymous with God's favor.

No one needs to feel guilty because they cannot afford to pay double digit compound interest rates. It is a worthy goal to pay back the principle you borrowed if you can do so, but neither you nor the lender should have presumed to know the future. If you cannot afford to repay the debt it simply means that both you and the lender were wrong in trying to foretell the future. After closing accounts and terminating the customer relationship with corporations, they are not rendering you any service that justifies their high double digit compound interest rates.

With interest rates at near historic lows for money deposited into savings accounts, how can bankers expect to make double digit compound interest rates? The "agreement" you made with them ends when you close your account. You terminate the agreement when you terminate your customer status. This is not a relationship you want to maintain, it is debt slavery. Unpaid debts are sold on the marketplace. Buying and selling debts is an industry in the United States but what is really being traded? Is it not the future labor of a human being? Isn't this trafficking in the bodies and souls of men?

If is very important for you to plan your financial affairs before embarking on the journey out of Babylon. Once you consult the laws that apply in the state where you reside, you know to budget to live on less than could be garnished from wages. Creditors can accept payments under a debt restructuring plan or third parties can accept a settlement offer, or they can take the matter to court to obtain a judgment in order to garnish wages. The portion of wages that can be taken is limited by applicable laws and you do not need to offer creditors more than the letter of the law requires. It is not more moral to pay off old debts than to provide for one's own household or give charity to the poor.

Some readers are likely to object, saying "but I gave my word." Who authorized you to make promises about the future? The moral failing was in presuming to know the future and making the promise. The wrong does not lie in leaving Babylon. Our culture is so saturated with reverence for Babylonian contract law that we esteem it more highly than God's commands. *He who does not care for his own is worse than an unbeliever* and *make it your ambition to work to give to those in need* are matters of morality. Scripture clearly indicates that none of us knows what the future holds, so we are never authorized to make promises about it.

Corporations certainly do not treat their own debts as moral issues. Even penalties and fines levied against corporations for harming people are treated as a cost of doing business. Having a debt reduced to a judgment is not a penalty for breaking a law or a fine, it does not mean you did something wrong. It is merely a method for the creditor to retain its right to collect while avoiding the statute of limitations that applies to debts.

Creditors cannot garnish wages without going to court and getting a judgment. If the creditor gets a judgment and garnishes your wages, your employer will be served with a court order and paperwork requiring it to hand over a specified sum of money. Garnishments are a complex mixture of state and federal statutes and for this reason might make the employer nervous. At the Federal level, the Consumer Credit Protection Act limits the amount of your earnings that are subject to garnishment. Generally the most that can be taken under federal law is 25 percent of disposable income or the amount that exceeds 30 times the Federal minimum wage, whichever is less.

Child support is an obligation that arises from natural law, in the words of an old time judge, "it has been man's duty to support his children since the first couple was expelled from the garden." Under federal law, up to 50 percent of a worker's disposable earnings can be garnished for child support and up to 60 percent if he is not supporting another spouse or child. An additional 5 percent could be taken to satisfy payments that are more than 12 weeks delinquent. Bankruptcy and tax court proceedings can be exempt from this 25 percent rule, but not from the 30 times the minimum wage provision. State law may allow workers to keep more of their wages and state law prevails.

In worse-case scenario, if an employer receives multiple garnishments notices, it is the employer's responsibility to make sure the total amount of money taken from wages does not exceed applicable limits. The employer can add a fee for handling the paperwork involved. The trend of making the employer responsible for employee finances goes along with withholdings for income tax. State law generally determines the priority in which garnishments should be paid. All other things being equal, garnishments are honored in the order they are received, except that obligations for child support have priority. Do not vent frustration on your employer for obeying a court order. In the very unlikely event you were not served with legal papers and did not get your day in court prior to wages being garnished, your remedy is to go to the court that entered the judgment and have it vacated for failure of service. If you can demonstrate the creditor could have served you but failed to do so, the court may forever bar it from seeking a judgment.

It is against federal law for an employer to fire an employee or treat them adversely on account of one garnishment. Multiple garnishments could be problematic as there is no specific statute protecting employees in this case. The best way to protect a job is by having an excellent work ethic, by doing work heartily as if it was being done for God. If an employee has a great attitude and work ethic, they employer is more likely to keep them on their payroll.

Although the government can take 15 percent of disposable wages for federally guaranteed student loans, it typically only takes 10 percent. For some students struggling to pay back student loans, this might come as good news. Understand what kinds of loans you took out to finance your education, were they federally insured? Talk to someone at the lending agency and work out an arrangement to the repayment terms at this rate so you can afford to live from day to day. If you are deeply in debt for student loans, prayerfully consider options like working in a troubled school district, on a remote reservation, joining one of the branches of the military, or entering another program that will repay the loans. Be realistic when you consider your options. It may be better to serve four years to become debt free than to spend the rest of your adult life in debt bondage. The federal government garnishes money for student loans after Medicare, state and federal taxes, and social security are withheld. It might even take its share after pension contributions are deducted. This is a reason to be sure that you are having the correct amount withheld for taxes. The government will take any tax refunds.

Consider the typical American family of four earning $50,233 a year. He makes $35,000 from his full time job. They are $18,654 dollars in debt, not including the mortgage on their home. They owe around $8,000 on credit cards and the rest for car loans. They are slowly sinking further into debt every year because they spend about $49,638 a year, which is more than their net income. They spend $16,920 a year on housing, including the mortgage and utilities. Utilities seem to creep up every year at a rate somewhat higher that wage increases. Housing is the largest single expense in their budget at 34.1 percent of their income. The cars cost $8,758 a year, 17.6 percent of their income. They spend $2,385 a year on co-pays and their share of a family medical policy through his job. A similar private policy could cost than over $1000 a month. They spend $6,133 per year on food and consume much of it away from home at the cost of $2,668 each year. Like other couples, they pay 17-20 percent interest monthly on the credit card debt. Each month they pay $240 on the cards, or 3 percent of the outstanding balance. Assume the couple has four cards and owes $2000 on each. Here is what is happening with each debt.

Principal: $2,000.
Interest: $33.33 ($2,000 x (1+20%/12))
Payment: $60 (3% of remaining balance)
Principal Repayment: $26.67
Remaining Balance: $1,973.33 ($2,000 - $26.67)

These calculations repeat monthly until balances are paid in full. This couple is actually paying only $60 a month toward the principal on the four credit cards and the rest of the payment goes toward interest. At this rate, the couple will pay $4,240 over 15 years to absolve the $2,000 on each of the four credit cards. Combine the cards and the couple will have paid $8,960 in interest along with $8000 in principle by making only minimum payments *if* they do not charge any more on the cards. The $240 a month the couple is paying on credit cards is 5.7 percent of their gross income. This does not include the interest the couple pays for the car loan. They borrowed $10,000 for 48 months at an interest rate of 7.05% to buy a used car. The payment is $239.46 a month. By the time they pay off the car, they will spend $11,494.08 for a $10,000 car that will have depreciated to being worth much less if they tried to sell it.

What happens to our average American couple if the wife loses her job or the husband loses his overtime? Assume the couple now brings home $30,000 a year. Adopting an austerity budget, they can turn down the thermostat down to save some of the fuel cost for heating the house, but the house still costs $16,000 a year. They stop eating in restaurants, but groceries still cost $4,500 a year. After much thought, they decide to keep her car so she can try and find another job, so the cars continue costing $7,000 per year. They can do little about the $2,385 for health care but pray they stay well. Even if they give up all recreational activities, stop buying any clothing (difficult to do with growing children) and postpone making home repairs, they really do not have money to make the minimum payments on the credit cards. They were paying $480 a month on debts for credit cards and cars, now they can only afford $300. The moral of this story is to never go into debt on two incomes.

America has achieved a unique status in the history of affluence as we have more cars than licensed drivers in this country. What about car debt? If this couple had saved the money they used to make the car payment at 3 percent interest for four years, they could have purchased a $10,000 car and had $2,195.00 in savings as a cushion for emergencies. The following example was adapted from a web site worth visiting, moneyhelpforchristians.com. It is an excellent resource.

> **Sally Saver** is a 30 year old who decides she will always make payments to herself of $239.46 per month and will always buy cars

that cost $10,000. She puts the money she saves into a high interest checking account that that yields 3%. She pays cash for a new used car every four years until she is 64 years old. During that time she will buy 9 cars. The first four years she drives a funky old car her parents gave her and uses public transportation when necessary. She buys her first car at age 34 – with cash.

Larry Impatient decides he will always buy cars costing $10,000 and finance them. At the age of 30 he goes out and gets his first car at a 7.05% loan with a payment of $239.46. He buys another used car every four years until he is 64 years old.

	Larry *Account Balance*	Sally *Auto Account Balance*
Car 1	$0	used old car
Car 2	$ 0	$ 2,195.00
Car 3	$ 0	$ 4,665.49
Car 4	$ 0	$ 7,446.05
Car 5	$ 0	$ 10,575.59
Car 6	$ 0	$ 14,097.92
Car 7	$ 0	$ 18,062.33
Car 8	$ 0	$ 22,524.31
Car 9	$ 0	$ 27,546.31

At age 64 Sally has $27,546.31 in a savings account and Larry has nothing. Most importantly, except for the first four year period, Larry and Sally drove the exact same cars.

How much should you spend on cars? The total cost, including car payments, gasoline, repairs and insurance should not be more than 15 percent of disposable income. According to one expert, the total value of the car you drive should never be worth more than half your take home pay. A gross salary of $50,000 provides about $35,000 take home, which means one $15,000 car or two $7,500 cars. How much it really costs to operate cars includes gas and oil, repairs, inspection, registration, insurance, and saving toward a replacement car. In this example, the most that these costs and payments should come to is about $437 a month.

Cars are a status symbol in America. Much advertising is devoted to getting us to think we need the newest and coolest vehicle. Try and remember that you cannot drive out of Babylon in car on which you are making payments. It is a new level of tragedy that cars are now being advertised to children as it has been determined they can influence their parents purchasing decisions. What do you want for your children? Do you want to raise them in debt bondage in Babylon or do you want them to be free?

Throwing off the Mark

Remember if you repent you must bring forth fruit in keeping with your repentance. If you take action to settle your debts and live living within your means, you will be on your way out of Babylon. Consumer debt is covered by positive law, rules enacted by human governments. *Render unto Caesar the things which are Caesar.* Corporations are creatures created by human government and their operations are governed by Caesar. It is legitimate to settle your debts using the laws which govern such matters. Corporations charging high interest rates are not operating under God's law. His statutes do not approve of usury, high compound interest rates. Satisfy creditors and settle debts using the means established under human laws. You are under no moral obligation to do more than law requires of you in these matters.

Having examined your financial situation, you know the total sum which you owe. Liquidate the debt as soon as possible, but do not feel obliged to pay creditors more than Caesar would let them have if they garnished your wages. Why should corporations get more than Caesar says? Perhaps you have equity in assets you can use to facilitate getting out of debt sooner. In planning to get out of Babylon, think carefully about shelter. Can you afford where you are currently living, or is it costing far more than a third of your disposable income? If the cost of shelter, including utilities, is too high consider downsizing or finding someone willing to share the expense. The strategies and plans you devise for getting out of debt as soon as possible ought to be as earnest as plans made by a slave working to purchase his freedom. You are in fact buying your financial freedom from debt bondage. The borrower is a slave to the lender is a statement about reality.

If you have repented of the folly of greed and presuming to be capable of predicting the future, you can live at peace. You have set your financial affairs right before the High King of Heaven. Now enjoy the peace of mind that comes with contentment. It is not a sin to be poor, but it is sinful to be greedy and covetous. Tragically greed has served as the basis of the United States economy for too long. As a nation, we are reaping the bitter consequences of what we have sown. Our national debt is alarmingly high and the interest rate on it is rising. This is a good reason to get yourself out of debt as soon as you possibly can.

The bankers might not like your repayment plan; they might want more than you can afford to give them. What you can afford to give them is a percent of your disposable income. This may be less than the minimum payment they want. If they will not restructure the debt and accept your repayment offer, they may default the debt and send it or sell it to a collection agency. Collection agencies can engage in annoying tactics, but this does not change what you can afford to pay. Do not waste money sending payments until they agree to settle the debt for what you can afford to pay. You do not need to take psychological abuse from strangers over the phone. Laws govern when collection agents can call you at home. You can decide whether or not to allow them to call you at work. If a creditor wrote off your account as uncollectible, feel free to treat is so yourself. The defaulted debt is already a black mark on your credit report for six years. If you never pay it will not look any worse on your credit report than it already does. Creditors seem less interested in having principle repaid than in making compound interest on debts. Creditors avail themselves to tax advantages by writing off accounts when they cannot charge usury interest rates. The laws regulating credit in the United States were enacted under heavy influence of bankers and other corporations. All you can do is the best you can do, after that, God has called you to peace.

Your goal is to pay off all your debts, except perhaps a mortgage, in three to five years. If you make less than the median income for your state, you should plan to pay off your debts in three years. If you make more than the median income, the plan can extend for five years. These time guidelines come from Chapter 13 of the federal Bankruptcy law. Begin by allocated 10 percent of disposable income towards debt liquidation. Set aside a similar amount for savings and for giving. Funds must be set aside for inevitable expenses such as car repairs, medical bills and eventually retirement, God willing. Remember, corporations are created and governed by human laws and you should submit yourself to such laws when it comes to repaying your debts. Scripture does not require you to do more than to be in subjection to the law. Consider the companies which purchase debts; this is what makes them part of the Babylonian system.

The company that invented the credit scoring system now sells psychological profiles on individuals to collection agencies. Psychological operations are being used against the American people and debt collectors are trained to use psychological profiling in their quest to collect. When the collection agent calls he is sitting in front of a computer screen which displays a rank ordered list of methods to use on a creditor. Beginning with the profile the program deems most likely to succeed, he will manipulate you using a strategy based on personality profile. If the first approach is not fruitful, he will move on to the one ranked as next most likely to succeed. The program uses data gleaned from many sources to make predictions about your personality. The exact algorithm the company uses is proprietary, naturally. Data for profiling comes from demographic data, internet searches, social networking services, and a host of other sources which is compiled in files by high speed computers. Programs are capable of searching for everything from a user name to emails, the style in which people write letters, their vocabulary, and items they purchase. This use of information is called data mining. Banks and credit card companies have access to millions of transactions a day, a great deal of data to be mined about people. Here is a marketing quote from one company offering selling this service, *"Just as credit scores are used by creditors to determine how good a credit risk you are. Psych scores confer predictive value for estimating how likely it is that someone behaves in a certain way."*

The United States military is forbidden to run psychological operations on American civilians, but corporations do so every day. Anything goes in Babylon in the name of the Almighty dollar and the sanctity of commercial transactions. Perhaps the program computes a profile that a debtor is a 'responsible citizen type' who feels badly about defaulting on a debt. The collection agent may engage in a strategy of sympathizing and feign interest in helping the debtor achieve the goal of paying off the debt. If the psychological profiling program indicates the debtor is a 'people person type' the collection agent may come across as being easily offended so the debtor will appease him. A corporation has no immortal soul, so it feels no guilt about manipulating you.

Can you see why talking to collection agents can lead to psychological distress? This is an intentional manipulation being perpetrated on the debtor. It has caused some people to become so dismayed and stressed out they resort to solving their financial problems by taking their own life. Profiling programs are psychological warfare being perpetrated against citizens. The data collected to assembly a profile for you is a feat of intelligence gathering. Have you ever paid for a visit to a doctor or a counselor with a credit card? Do you use a store loyalty card at the grocery store? Where does the data collected reside? Last time you purchased tires, were they the top of the line or a discount brand? We leave an electronic trail when we use plastic or surf the internet. This is the reality of modern life. Should corporations be using this data to monitor your personal life and assemble a dossier on you? If you do not find this an outrageous invasion of privacy, it may be because you do not comprehend the magnitude of the problem we face. We live in a nation where the right to terminate the life of a fetus is granted under some constitutional right to privacy, so how can lives of adults be invaded with no regard for privacy? Our constitution gives us the right to be secure in our persons and papers, meaning our government cannot access documents and data on our personal affairs without due process and probable cause. How do multinational corporations manage to access our data? Did you authorize anyone to engage in psychological warfare against you by using your information?

The practice of profiling based on purchasing habits is relatively recent trend. According to an article which appeared in the *New York Times*, it started when a math-loving corporate executive decided to analyze all the data his company collected about what cardholders were buying. He found out purchasing behavior could serve as a sort of window into the soul. For instance, people who buy generic oil are more likely to miss a credit card payment than people who purchase brand name oil. Everything from how often and the time of day you log into online accounts, to what you buy at the store is part of a massive online data base. Bits can be assembled to predict whether you are anxious or might be short of cash.

The Internal Revenue has assisted this process by creating merchant codes to distinguish between goods and services. A weekend of folly might be coded:

5921 Package Stores-Beer, Wine, and Liquor
5813 Drinking Places
7995 Betting/Casino Gambling
5813 Drinking Places
7273 Dating/Escort Services
3501-3790 Hotels/Motels/Inns/Resorts
9223 Bail and Bond Payments
8111 Legal Services, Attorneys
5912 Drug Stores and Pharmacies

On the other hand, a mission trip to Haiti to help victims of the earthquake might look like this:

4112 Passenger Railways
3000-3299 Airlines
4821 Telegraph Services
5976 Orthopedic Goods - Prosthetic Devices
6300 Insurance
7395 Photo Developing

The system of codes was initially designed to help the tax assessor to determine if payments were for services performed by an individual who would need to report them as income, or if the purchases were for goods. In the words of our tax code, "If a person is engaged in a trade or business and, in the course of that trade or business, pays any person $600 or more of rent, salaries, wages, premiums, annuities, compensation, remunerations, emoluments, or other fixed or determinable gains, profits, and income during a calendar year, section 6041 generally requires the payer to file an information return with the Internal Revenue Service (Service) and to furnish an information statement to the payee." The corporations have been collecting data, but when were they ever authorized to share it with one another or to use it to manipulate customers?

The man calling from the collection agency about your

debt believes he knows the most efficient way to manipulate you into sending him money. He does not care where you get it, whether it is the milk money for the baby or a donation you set aside to feed widows in Africa. His is using a computer generated strategy to help him achieve his goal. Neither the collection agent nor the program cares that you are doing as much, if not more, than justice demands. If you get behind on a mortgage and loose the roof over your head, neither the collection agent nor program cares. The program doesn't care because it is incapable of carrying; it is simply a string of code. The agent probably cares more about his financial plight than you and may be very cynical about people. He probably does not care and even if he does, he is simply an agent for an entity that exists for the purpose of maximizing profits for its shareholders.

Since making money is all corporations understand, the best way to communicate effectively with them is by not being their valued customer. When any business treats you arbitrarily or unfairly, raising interest rates or assessing penalties for late payment because it changed a due date, call and ask for the fees to be waived or to restore the original rate you agreed to when you opened the account. If you are struggling financially, call lenders and ask to have interest rates reduced. This is reasonable because the company is getting very low interest rates on money it borrows from the Federal Reserve Board. If reasonable requests like these are not honored, close your accounts and follow up with a letter. Take your business elsewhere. Explain the terms under which you will repay the outstanding balance on the account and include those terms in the letter closing the account. The letter needs to confirm all the details of the phone conversation. Explain why you will no longer do business with the company. Save a copy of the letter and be sure you send it to the correct address. If you close a department store credit card, you also need to stop shopping at the store. It is imperative that American citizens begin exercising the little economic power we still possess to bring the corporations inline while it is even remotely possible. There is very little time left for our economic decisions to have any impact on corporations because they are all becoming multinationals and making money elsewhere. What material object to you need so badly that you are willing to be abused to acquire it?

Banks are obviously concerned that citizens are no longer cowering in fear of bad credit scores because they are engaged an expensive propaganda campaign intended to make us care about credit scores. That is why we are being subjected to the goofy, but memorable commercials. Advertisements are an expense, so they must be deemed both necessary and effective. There are web sites designed to teach consumers the importance of having good credit scores. Remember, a good credit score means are willing to go deeply into debt, to make high minimum payments, and pay a great deal of interest for many years. Good for the companies lending money, not so good for you. A good credit score means you will make a great debt slave!

The worst thing about having a poor credit score is that you won't be able to borrow money. In the end this will be a blessing. If you cannot borrow additional sums of money, it is only a matter of time until you dig your way out of debt and enjoy freedom, financial and mental. In time, you will be out of Babylon. You need to care about your integrity and character; but these are far from synonymous with a credit score. A credit score is a number assigned which rates your value as a debtor, an economic slave who labors to profit another. If you have a poor score, it means you are not a good debtor. Is your goal in life being a good debtor so bankers will make a lot of money from you? Do you want to borrow large sums of money at high interest rates and work two jobs to pay for junk made by slave labor in the developing world? Is this how you wanted to spend your life?

Perhaps you are persuaded of the wisdom of avoiding debt for consumer goods, but are concerned about how you will ever afford a mortgage for a house without a good credit score. How did your grandparents get their first house? Likely they saved a substantial down payment so the lender was certain the property itself would be adequate security for the loan. In the old days, it was the house, not the borrower that served as security for a loan on real property. The property, not the person, should be the security for a loan for real estate. All across American people are learning this to their sorrow. People borrowed more money to purchase property than it was worth and the bubble burst, leaving them with upside down mortgages. A great number of Americans owe more on their homes than they are worth in today's market. If you are in this situation, forget what the house is worth as an investment and consider the more practical issue. Does it meet your need for shelter and can you afford what you are paying for it? If these things are true, be content.

The individuals who scammed the American public and stole billions of dollars by inflating the price of homes and then deflating real estate will eventually give an account for their deeds. Meanwhile, you are in a home and if you can afford it, be content. If you don't own a home and think it would be prudent to have one, consider purchasing it from its human owner on a contract for deed. A contract for deed means the buyer makes payments until the property is completely paid for, and then gets the deed. If the buyer defaults, the seller gets to keep his property and them money paid. The property is the security for financing its purchase. How much interest should you pay the seller in this arrangement? Consider splitting the difference between what the seller cold make on money in a savings account and what a mortgage from a bank would cost the borrower. The borrower will still need to come up with a substantial down payment to offer the seller who will be moving on. Many people in American cannot afford to stay in their homes and they cannot figure out how to get out of them. Find someone in this situation and make them an offer.

Be wary of signing up with credit services recommended on bank web sites as these may merely be fronts for banks. There is nothing a business can do for you that you cannot do for yourself in these matters. You do not need to pay someone else to handle your creditors; or you may be paying creditors and paying for the "help" too. There are a few reputable non-profit consumer credit counseling services that can be very helpful. Check to make sure that you are dealing with one of them. A legitimate non-profit consumer credit counseling service will do a complete financial assessment and will make you cut up your credit cards if they are going to help you. You will send them one payment a month, pay a small monthly fee, and they will make payments to your creditors. Given their experience and expertise, they might be able to negotiate a better plan than you can manage with a group of creditors. They might also inform you that they cannot help you because you are too far in debt for them to be of service, in which case they will recommend bankruptcy. Should you consider bankruptcy? If a non-profit consumer credit counseling service recommends this because you cannot reasonably pay off your debts within the statute of limitations creditors are willing to accept, talk to a reputable bankruptcy attorney about your situation. Remember, this legal provision was created along with the rest of the body of law in the United States and it is based on biblical principles. Study the Old Testament and you will learn that when God was king over Israel, no one was in debt service for more than seven years.

If you borrowed money thinking the future would be better, you were presumptuous and so were the lenders. Do what you must to get out of debt. If your creditors refuse to restructure your debts and will not accept a settlement offer, you may have no alternative for getting out of debt but to declare bankruptcy. Unlike the Federal Reserve, you cannot create money out of thin air. You cannot keep borrowing money. You must save money. These are the core principles for living outside of Babylon. If you declare bankruptcy it will put a black mark on your credit report for ten years. This may affect everything from the price of your automobile insurance to how a landlord feels about renting an apartment to you. There is almost no consequence of having a poor credit score that is not overcome by having real money in a savings account. A landlord who is hesitant to rent to you because of a poor credit score is likely to reconsider a tenant who is willing to triple his damage deposit. The fuel oil company reluctant to do business with a customer with a poor score will almost certainly accept a cash prepayment for the winter's bill.

Whether you have a good credit score or a poor one, you are still marked by the beast. Worshipping the beast means cowering before the giver of the score, the world's financial system. A prostitute allows herself to be used and abused for money and other material goods. Stop prostituting yourself for Mammon. How could the illustration be any clearer in Revelation? We are all appalled at modern day slavery and the idea of women being trafficked and abused but need to realize the psychological and spiritual abuse we endure in Babylon.

Consider adding a personal statement to your credit report revoking the use of your social security number for commercial transactions. Most likely corporations will simply ignore it, but you can make it. Consider freezing your credit report so it cannot be viewed without your permission. We need to be creative and find ways to assert our humanity in the face of the beast. Refuse to be treated as a commodity. You are an immortal spirit created in the image of the living God. Stop cowering in fear before a beast created by man. Get everyone you know to read this book and take action. We need a mass exodus out of Babylon.

The New Covenant

This chapter is written for readers who believe the bible is authoritative for life here on earth. Christians in the United States have embraced beliefs about money based more on the commercial practices of ancient Babylon than those from the kingdom of heaven. Escaping from the grip of the Babylonian mindset requires rethinking many assumptions about wealth in light of diligent study of instructions from heaven. We cannot simply accept without questioning what the world's culture dictates to us, for *where a man's treasure is, there is his heart also.* Each individual believer must arrive at a set of convictions by which to govern his life, and this is as true of financial affairs as it is in other realms of life. Indeed this area of life is of urgent concern since the *cares and anxieties of the world and the deceitfulness of riches can choke out the Word of God.*

In general Americans believe in the Almighty dollar and we are a people who treat contracts as nearly sacred. In the Christian community, it is widely assumed Christians are morally bound to honor the terms of a contract *no matter what the consequences.* In Babylon, contracts were sworn with solemn oaths in temples with pagan priests as witnesses. A contract is, however, nothing but an agreement set down in writing. Both parties to the agreement are supposed to be operating in good faith and neither party ought to violate public policy. Have bankers and multinational corporations been operating in good faith the last few years? Or have their actions been completely motivated to increase corporate profits while ruining the world's economy?

Earlier we looked at ancient Babylonian rules regarding commerce and contracts. An important ruler from that civilization, Hammurabi, set forth one of the earliest legal codes. His code recognized three classes of people, the elites, the slaves, and *mushkenu*. Slaves were recognizable by the identification mark branded or tattooed on their arm. Normal citizens of Babylon could become slaves as debts were secured by the person of the debtor. How does this differ from owing money on a credit card if all a person can afford to do is make the minimum payment each month for a lifetime? Year after year he will be paying interest on the debt without ever paying off the principal because of compound interest. The person who owes $5000 at 18 percent interest can pay $100 a month for 35 years and thus pay more than $12,000 in interest on the debt. Until the debt is paid off, the person runs the risk of having a bad credit score, a black mark attached to his name, if he misses a payment or even makes a late payment. Since the credit card debt is not secured by any tangible property, isn't the debt secured by the person of the debtor? Doesn't this system reduce the debtor to the status of a salve?

Much can be leaned by a study of the parable of the shrewd manager described in Luke's gospel (16:1-15). Jesus's conclusion to this parable was this, *what is highly valued among men is detestable in God's sight.* In the Lord's sample prayer we learn that God forgives us our debts as we forgive our debtors (Matthew 6:12). Debt forgiveness is a theme that runs throughout the scriptures. Jesus told parables on this topic. Clearly the new covenant is about grace and forgiveness, not extracting the letter of the law.

The real problem with entering into a contract to repay a debt with future earnings is more fundamental than signing a contract, entering into an agreement, or giving one's word. The real problem originates with the arrogant assumption we know what the future holds. Consider the attitude we are admonished to have about the future which is articulated in James 4:13-15.

> *Now listen, you who say, "Today or tomorrow we will go to this or that city, spend a year there, carry on business and make money." Why, you do not even know what will happen tomorrow. What is your life? You are a mist that appears for a little while and then vanishes. Instead, you ought to say, "If it is the Lord's will, we will live and do this or that."*

We lack the capacity to enter into binding agreements about the future because we cannot foresee what it holds. It is in God's hands, not ours. We simply do not know what will happen tomorrow. This is a simple principle. How can we agree to pay money to someone in the future when we do not know whether we will even be on earth next week? Jesus advised us to always let our 'yes' be 'yes' and our 'no' be 'no.' He was talking about matters we could testify to as fact, things in the present or past. He was not suggesting that we could predict the future. Jesus was not talking about honoring contracts, but about truthfulness. We can only be truthful about what we know already. Ideally we are to *owe nothing to any man but love*. We should not be borrowing money to buy things we do not need and we should not have to in the kingdom of God where all are admonished to work to *give to those in need*. Within the kingdom of heaven there is no place for lending money to the poor, but plenty of opportunity to give to them. *Whoever is kind to the poor lends to the LORD, and He will reward them for what they have done* (Proverbs 19:17).

When God set forth laws for the nation of Israel, He addressed the issue of debts. The longest any Israelite could be in debt was seven years, because at the end of every seven years, debts were cancelled. The Israelites were told they should give generously to the poor and to do so without a grudging heart because the Lord would bless the giver in all his work and in everything he put his hands to (See Deuteronomy 15:10.) God recognized there would always be poor and needy people in the world.

Modern day lenders violate scriptural principles by charging the highest interest rates to those in the worse financial difficulties. Companies make high profits lending money to those in dire financial difficulties who are about to go under. Individuals are charged interest rates of 27 percent and more. High compound interest rates enslave people. When a person must work for years in an attempt to pay back significantly more money than the original sum borrowed, he is a debt slave. Banks are charging rates as high as 59.9 percent APR. At this rate, an individual making the minimum monthly payment on $500 would never repay the debt.

The Federal Reserve recently said that consumer credit card debt in the United States totaled $880 billion. This figure when adjusted to current dollars shows an increase of a hundred-fold in the last 40 years. Why? Perhaps citizens were trapped into living on credit by assuming we would be more prosperous in the future than we are today, or perhaps it was because inflation leads us to believe we repay with dollars that are worth less in the future. We borrowed from the future and now we cannot afford to repay debts and meet current expenses. Our economy is in serious trouble. Visit the web site www.usdebtclock.org and you can see the problem. The average debt per taxpayer for the national debt is more than $127,156. The total debt for each family stands at $681,645 and it is growing daily.

Clearly lending money to the poor at outrageous interest rates violates God's expressed ideals. Credit card companies reserve for themselves the right to change terms of contracts. Companies employ teams of lawyers to write fine print regular people who did not graduate from Harvard law school are not likely to understand, using terms like "universal default." Universal default provisions allowed lender A to raise interest rates on an existing debt to its default rate if the borrower defaulted with lender B. About half of companies offering credit cards included universal default provisions in their contracts until this heinous practice was outlawed in 2009. Given the way credit scores are computed, the practice continues because a default affects credit scores, and credit scores are used to determine interest rates.

Credit card companies are among the biggest campaign contributors in federal elections, passing out more money to candidates of all political persuasions than do the oil and big pharmaceutical companies. Credit card companies are in the business of creating money by issuing credit. The US constitution gives Congress the exclusive right to create money for the nation, but Congress no longer exercises that right and responsibility. It is far beyond the scope of this book to explain where the money loaned comes from, but basically it is created out of nothing. For every dollar that grandma has deposited in her passbook savings account, the bank may be lending out $100. The banks are now in control of our economic system, rather than our Congress being in control of it. Our founding fathers were very concerned about building protections into our form of government to keep banks from getting power over the American people. This is why they expressly gave Congress the right to issue money, but only allowed gold and silver to be legal tender in payment of debts. This provision would have prevented banks from inflating the money supply. Now that our money is not tied to anything tangible, credit card companies make money by selling the future. We now face the grim consequence of this practice. Think about the price of an ounce of gold now compared to what it was worth when the constitution was written, the difference between the two figures is inflation.

We spend less now than our parent's did on basics such as clothing, food, and appliances once dollars are adjusted for inflation. We spend more on housing and much more on medical care. Consider the typical American family with both parents in the work force. A medium income family has 75 percent more money than its parents after money is adjusted for inflation. But after the couple makes the mortgage payment, shells out money for mandatory health insurance, pays for the two cars needed so both parents can commute to work, and pays for childcare, they have less money than their parents had available for spending. Our situation has not improved, but these factors might contribute to the increase in use of antidepressants and rate of teenage pregnancies.

Consumer credit laws in the United States were modeled on biblical principles through the twentieth century. States set limits on the interest rates consumers could be charged. The whole nature of borrowing and lending changed when the corporations discovered that consumers in trouble were extremely profitable. People in desperate straits will agree to paying high interest rates in the hope things will be different in the future. This is, of course, unrealistic thinking. Wages are not going to increase 28.99 or 59.00 percent in the next two years, interest rates being charged to the poor among us. Once mathematical adjustments are done for inflation, the real increase in wages in the United States has only been 1 percent over the past thirty years.

Taking a loan is a type of time travel, using tomorrow's wages to pay for an item desired today. The only way this item can be paid for in the future is for the borrower to live on less money in the future than in the present. It is extremely unlikely there will be significantly more money in the future than today. Probably the only thing we can depend on about the financial future is that taxes will increase, the cost of fuel will increase, and inflation will gobble up the 1 percent increase in wages we might see over the next three decades.

The bible recognizes the practice of borrowing and how lenders should conduct themselves.

> *When you make a loan of any kind to your neighbor, do not go into his house to get what he is offering as a pledge. Stay outside and let the man to whom you are making the loan bring the pledge out to you. If the man is poor, do not go to sleep with his pledge in your possession. Return his cloak to him by sunset so that he may sleep in it. Then he will thank you, and it will be regarded as a righteous act in the sight of the Lord your God.* (Deuteronomy 24:10-13.)

> *If you lend money to one of my people among you who is needy, do not be like a moneylender; charge him no interest. If you take your neighbor's cloak as a pledge, return it to him by sunset, because his cloak is the only covering he has for his body. What else will he sleep in? When he cries out to me, I will hear, for I am compassionate.* (Exodus 22:25-27)

We are now a nation of slaves as *the borrower becomes a slave to the lender*, psychologically this is true and it is literally becoming true as well.

The wicked borrows, and does not repay, but the righteous shows mercy, and gives (Psalm 35:31). If you borrowed money with no intention of repaying it was wicked, it was a con job. If you borrowed money thinking you were going to have more money tomorrow than you have today, you were the victim of a con job, you were naïve. If you borrowed money thinking you could predict the future, you were foolish and did not listen to

God. The lender who used a credit score to predict your ability to repay was foolish as well. None of us can know the future.

Does the scripture offer examples of individuals re-negotiating debts and settlements for less than the amount owed? It certainly does. God offered his people a way to square up their economic situation:

> *At the end of every seven years you must cancel debts. This is how it is to be done: Every creditor shall cancel the loan he has made to his fellow Israelite. He shall not require payment from his fellow Israelite or brother, because the LORD's time for canceling debts has been proclaimed.*
> Deuteronomy 15:1-2 (NIV)

When God was King, He mandated release from debts every seven years. Based on this principle, arrive at a debt settlement arrangement to be debt free in the next three to five years. This time frame assumes you have paid on debts for some years already. Debt settlement is a legal agreement between a debtor and a creditor where a portion of the debtor's debt is simply "forgiven." This might be the best way for creditors to get the money from people who are in economic distress. If you and the creditor can arrive at an agreement what you are doing is moral according to the scripture. It would only be wicked to enter into an agreement for debt settlement if you borrowed money with no intention of ever repaying it, in which case you are being deceitful. If you have been making payments on your debts, clearly it was not your intention to avoid repaying debts. There is a difference between being incapable and being unwilling.

The scripture considers lending money to the poor at high interest rates to be morally reprehensible. It may have been foolish for you to take the bait offered by the bankers, but it was immoral for them to offer unsecured credit at high interest rates. With bankers racking up wealth by charging interest rates, adding on fees, increasing minimum payments and lowering credit limits, the combined effect can trigger interest rates as high as the outlawed universal default rates because of the impact on credit scores. These practices are simply a sophisticated form of debt bondage.

If you have repented of not being content and borrowing against a future you cannot predict, you are at liberty to correct your finances and have peace of mind. Peace of mind will only come to you when you are willing to live within your means and accept each day as it comes.

> *Better to have little, with fear for the LORD, than to have great treasure and inner turmoil.* (Proverbs 15:16.)

> *Better is the little of the righteous than the abundance of many wicked.* (Proverbs 37:16.)

> *Come now, you rich, weep and howl for your miseries which are coming upon you. Your riches have rotted and your garments have become moth-eaten. Your gold and your silver have rusted; and their rust will be a witness against you and will consume your flesh like fire. It is in the last days that you have stored up your treasure! Behold, the pay of the laborers who mowed your fields, and which has been withheld by you, cries out against you; and the outcry of those who did the harvesting has reached the ears of the Lord of Sabbath. You have lived luxuriously on the earth and led a life of wanton pleasure; you have fattened your hearts in a day of slaughter.* (James 5:1-5)